C O N T E N T S

D1550642

Baked Grouper
with Creole Sauce—page 43

WHAT IS CONVECTION COOKING AND HOW DOES IT WORK?

In a convection oven, a fan circulates hot air around the food to distribute it evenly throughout the cavity. The Precise Air™ convection system utilizes an innovative fan that reverses direction for optimal distribution of air and heat circulation for convection baking and convection roasting. The frequency with which the convection fan changes direction and the amount of time for which the fan is off (not turning) depends on the convection cooking mode selected. Some modes will reverse the fan frequently for optimal performance while other modes may not reverse the fan at all.

Convection Bake Multi (some models) allows for more than one rack of food to bake evenly in about the same time as one rack of the same item in traditional bake. Convection Bake 1-Rack (some models) is optimized to cook one rack of food (lasagna, cookies, biscuits, etc.) evenly and quickly. For models with only one Convection Bake option, multiple racks and individual racks of food may be cooked. Most convection baking requires a 25°F temperature reduction for optimal performance. (See Auto Recipe™ Conversion on page 5).

Convection Roast is designed to roast meats and poultry with a golden, browned outside, and tender, juicy inside. Convection Roasting, does not require a temperature reduction and cooking time can be reduced up to 25%.

The following pages provide useful information and cooking on convection cooking.

ADVANTAGES AND BENEFITS OF CONVECTION COOKING

Convection Baking and Roasting provide a number of advantages over traditional cooking:

1. Large quantities of food can be prepared at one time in a convection oven because the circulating air evenly distributes the heat. Multiple racks of food, such as biscuits, cookies, and appetizers, can be prepared at one time in preparation for special events or holidays.
2. Food can be cooked faster. Convection Roasting decreases the time required to cook meats and poultry while browning them and sealing in the juices. Convection Baking allows for multiple racks of food to be cooked at once, reducing the time normally spent baking one rack at a time.
3. Time and money are saved because larger food quantities are cooked in Convection Bake at lower temperatures in a shorter amount of time, saving energy.

Conventional baking temperatures generally require a 25°F reduction in temperature when using Convection Bake. See the Owner's Manual for design and feature information concerning your particular oven model.

Preheating the oven is recommended prior to Convection Baking. However, when convection roasting meats, preheating the oven is not typically required. Each recipe indicates when a preheated oven is required and when it is not. Follow recipe instructions when Convection Baking or Roasting for optimal results.

Some package instructions for frozen casseroles or main dishes have been developed using commercial convection ovens. For best results in this oven, adapt the conventional baking directions for Convection Baking.

When cooking on one rack, check food at minimum times or earlier. The convection system will cook multiple racks of food in approximately the same time as conventional baking with a single rack.

The same cookware and bakeware that are normally used when conventionally baking can also be used in convection ovens. For best results, use shiny aluminum or silver-colored cookware.

Dark or matte finish cookware will produce darker browning on food surfaces. Do not use cookware lined with aluminum foil as it reflects heat away from the food and may increase cooking times.

Use pans with low sides whenever possible. A shallow pan allows air to circulate around the food more efficiently.

Heat-resistant paper and plastic containers that manufacturers recommend for use in conventional ovens can be used in convection ovens. Oven-safe plastic cookware is also suitable for use in the convection oven when used according to cookware package directions.

CONVECTION BAKING

Multi-Rack Convection Baking

Because of the even air circulation in a convection oven, food can be baked with superior results on two or three racks at a time. Multi-rack baking may increase cooking times slightly for some foods, but since 2 to 3 racks of food are being cooked simultaneously the overall result is substantial time savings. Oven cavity and rack configurations vary from model to model, so for the proper rack and pan placement in your oven model, refer to the Owner's Manual.

One-Rack Convection Baking

When increased quantities are not required, one-rack baking provides excellent results for larger items such as casseroles and lasagnas, often cooking them in a shorter period of time. Oven cavity and rack configuration vary from model to model, so for the proper rack and pan placement in your oven model, refer to the Owner's Manual.

Auto Recipe™ Conversion

Some models are equipped with Auto Recipe™ conversion. When this feature is engaged the oven automatically reduces your standard baking temperature by 25°F. The recipes in this cookbook have both the conventional baking temperature and the converted convection baking temperature. Enter the converted temperature (in parentheses) if Auto Recipe™ conversion is disabled or not present on this oven model. Refer to your Owner's Manual for additional information on this feature.

When baking on 3 racks, space the racks to divide the oven evenly. Some models require the use of an offset rack. Refer to your Owner's Manual for more details on the actual rack positions and racks to use.

For two-rack baking, place the racks evenly spaced toward the center of the oven. Refer to your Owner's Manual for more details on the actual rack positions and the racks to use.

Allow 4 to 5 inches between pans when baking loaves of yeast breads, quick breads or loaf cake for best circulation of heated air.

When baking four cake layers, four pies or four loaves of bread, stagger pan placement on two racks (as shown) for best browning.

Roasts cooked in a convection oven are well browned with tender, juicy interiors. In the Convection Roast mode, preheating is not required. In most cases, cooking times will be less in the convection oven than in a conventional oven. Check food after the minimum cook time has passed. To assure the desired degree of doneness, use the oven meat probe provided with the oven and the Convection Roast setting. See the following page for internal temperatures. The broil pan and special roasting rack (some models), provided with your GE oven allows heated air to circulate over and under the roast. As a result, roasts are deliciously browned on all sides. Refer to your Owner's Manual for additional information on the broil pan and roasting rack associated with your oven.

To insert probe, measure the distance to the center of the roast by laying the temperature probe on top of the meat. Mark with thumb and forefinger where the edge of the meat comes on the probe.

Insert the probe horizontally up to the point marked off with your finger. Make sure that tip of probe is in the center of meat. Once the meat is done roasting, remove the probe from the meat. Leave the probe attached to the receptacle in the oven wall until the oven cools. Then remove the probe and clean. Because of variation in oven cavity design, location of the probe receptacle may differ from model to model. Refer to the Owner's Manual for information concerning your particular model.

ADAPTING RECIPES FOR CONVECTION BAKING AND CONVECTION ROASTING

1. As a general rule to follow when converting recipes for Convection Baking, reduce baking temperatures by 25°F. When Convection Roasting the baking temperature is not reduced.

2. Some convection oven models have a multi-rack and 1-rack convection bake option. Multi-rack convection bake allows for two or more racks of food to be cooked evenly at once. The 1-rack convection bake option is designed for optimal cooking and browning one rack of food. Models with only one Convection Bake mode are designed to cook food on either one rack or multiple racks. Refer to your Owner's Manual for detailed information on your particular model.

3. Preheating is not necessary when Convection Roasting, but it is recommended for Convection Baking.

4. Cook times may be reduced. Some foods may actually cook in $1/4$ to $1/3$ less time in the convection oven. Check foods for doneness at or before minimum cooking time.

5. Use the pan size and type recommended by the recipe.

6. Some convection oven models are equipped with Auto Recipe™ conversion feature. Refer to the Owner's Manual for detailed information on your particular model.

BROILING

1. Always use broiler pan and rack that comes with the oven. It is designed to minimize smoking and splattering by trapping juices in the shielded lower part of the pan.
2. Slice or slit fat evenly around outside edges of steaks and chops to prevent curling during broiling. Use tongs when turning meat to prevent piercing meat and losing juices.
3. If desired, marinate meats or chicken before broiling. Brush with sauce or marinade during last five minutes only. Refer to your Owner's Manual for more information on broiling times and rack positions.

Tasty Chicken Bites
with Tarragon-Mustard Sauce–page 10

TASTY CHICKEN BITES WITH TARRAGON-MUSTARD SAUCE

MAKES 6 TO 8 SERVINGS

Ingredients

CHICKEN BITES

- 1 cup dry bread crumbs
- 1/2 cup grated Parmesan cheese
- 1/2 teaspoon thyme
- 1/4 teaspoon salt
- 1/2 teaspoon lemon pepper
- 1/4 teaspoon garlic powder
- 1/2 cup melted butter
- 6 skinless, boneless chicken breasts, cut into 1 1/2 inch cubes

TARRAGON-MUSTARD SAUCE

- 1 cup sour cream
- 1/4 cup Dijon mustard
- 1/2 teaspoon tarragon
- 1/2 teaspoon sugar
- 1/4 teaspoon hot pepper sauce

Preparation

CHICKEN BITES

- Preheat oven in Convection Bake to 375°F (*350°F).
- Combine bread crumbs, Parmesan cheese, thyme, salt, lemon pepper and garlic powder. Mix well.
- Dip chicken cubes in butter and coat evenly with crumb mixture. Place coated chicken pieces on baking sheet.
- Convection Bake for 15 to 20 minutes or until done.
- Serve with Tarragon-Mustard Sauce.

TARRAGON-MUSTARD SAUCE

- Combine Tarragon-Mustard Sauce ingredients in a 2-cup glass measuring cup. Microwave on HIGH for 1 minute or until heated.

SUGAR AND SPICE WALNUTS

MAKES 1 POUND

Ingredients

- 1/2 cup melted butter
- 1 cup firmly packed light brown sugar
- 1 teaspoon cinnamon
- 1 lb. walnut halves (about 4 cups)

Preparation

- Preheat oven in Convection Bake to 350°F (*325°F).
- In 3-quart casserole, combine melted butter, brown sugar and cinnamon. Microwave on HIGH for 2 to 3 minutes, until thickened or syrupy, stirring often.
- Add nuts and mix to coat. Spread walnuts on baking sheet.
- Convection Bake for 10 to 12 minutes.
- Spread on wax paper to cool. Refrigerate in airtight container.

*Note: Enter this temperature if your oven does not reduce the oven convection temperature automatically by 25°F in the display.

MINI-CHEDDAR APPETIZERS

Ingredients

- 1/4 cup finely chopped sun-dried tomatoes
- 4 cups shredded cheddar cheese
- 4 beaten eggs
- 1/3 cup milk
- 1/4 cup dry bread crumbs
- 1/4 cup chopped green onion
- 60 mini phyllo dough pastry shells

Preparation

- Preheat oven in Convection Bake to 375°F (*350°F).
- Reconstitute tomatoes, if necessary, according to package directions. Drain well and chop.
- Combine all ingredients. Mix well. Divide the mixture evenly between the mini pastry shells.
- Convection Bake for 25 to 35 minutes or until browned, puffed and set in center.
- Serve warm.

Cooking Option

Spread mixture in a lightly greased 8-inch square baking dish. After baking, cut into squares.

ARTICHOKE DIP

Ingredients

- 1 (14 oz.) can drained and finely chopped artichoke hearts
- 1 cup mayonnaise
- 1 cup grated Parmesan cheese
- 1/4 teaspoon garlic salt
  Paprika

Preparation

- Preheat oven in Convection Bake to 375°F (*350°F).
- In 8-inch square baking dish, mix chopped artichokes with mayonnaise, Parmesan cheese and garlic salt. Sprinkle with paprika.
- Convection Bake for 15 to 20 minutes or until heated through and top is light brown.

BARBECUE BABY BACK RIBS

Ingredients

- 2 lbs. baby back ribs, cut in serving size pieces
- 1 chopped medium onion
- 2 cups hot water
  Bottled barbecue sauce

Preparation

- Preheat oven in Convection Bake to 375°F (*350°F).
- Place ribs, onion and water in shallow baking dish. Cover.
- Convection Bake for 40 minutes.
- Remove excess water and pour barbecue sauce over ribs.
- Continue baking, uncovered, 20 to 30 minutes or until tender.

*Note: Enter this temperature if your oven does not reduce the oven convection temperature automatically by 25°F in the display.

SAUSAGE SPIRALS

Spread sausage mixture down the center of dough.

Cut each roll into 4 slices and arrange on baking sheet.

Ingredients

- ½ lb. lean bulk sausage
- ⅓ cup chopped onion
- 1 tablespoon catsup
- 1 teaspoon fresh lemon juice
- ½ teaspoon Italian seasoning
- ¼ teaspoon garlic powder
- 1 (8 oz.) pkg. crescent rolls
- 1 beaten egg

Preparation

- Preheat oven in Convection Bake to 375°F (*350°F).
- Saute sausage and onion over medium-high heat until meat is browned. Drain. Stir in catsup, lemon juice, Italian seasoning and garlic powder. Set aside to cool.
- Divide pastry into 4 rectangles and press on seams to make a solid piece. Divide sausage mixture into fourths. Spread sausage mixture onto dough to within ½-inch of one long edge.
- Brush this long edge of pastry with beaten egg and roll dough toward this edge, pressing edge of roll to seal. Brush egg on all sides of each roll. Cut each roll into fourths. Place rolls cut side down on baking sheet.
- Convection Bake for 9 to 12 minutes or until rolls have desired browning.

TINY CHICKEN TURNOVERS

MAKES ABOUT 20 APPETIZERS

Ingredients

- ½ (8 oz.) pkg. softened cream cheese
- ½ cup softened butter
- 1 cup all-purpose flour
- 1 cup finely chopped cooked chicken
- 1 tablespoon finely chopped onion
- 1 tablespoon finely chopped sweet red pepper
- 2 tablespoons mayonnaise
- 1 teaspoon Dijon mustard
- ¼ teaspoon salt
- ⅛ teaspoon white pepper
- 1 beaten egg

Preparation

- Preheat oven in Convection Bake to 400°F (*375°F).
- Beat cream cheese and butter together until light and fluffy. Blend in flour to make a soft dough. Turn onto floured surface and knead lightly 10 to 12 strokes. Wrap in plastic wrap and refrigerate until firm enough to handle.
- Combine chicken, onion, red pepper, mayonnaise, mustard, salt and pepper; blend thoroughly. Set aside while rolling out dough.
- Roll dough on well-floured surface to ¹/₁₆-inch thickness. Cut into 3-inch rounds.
- Place one heaping teaspoon of filling on each pastry round. Brush edges of pastry with egg. Fold pastry rounds in half over filling. Seal edges together with a fork. Brush tops with remaining egg.
- Convection Bake for 13 to 16 minutes or until golden.

***Note:** Enter this temperature if your oven does not reduce the oven convection temperature automatically by 25°F in the display.*

COCKTAIL REUBENS

Ingredients

36 slices toasted cocktail rye bread

1/2 cup Thousand Island dressing

1 (8 oz.) can rinsed and drained sauerkraut

1/4 lb. thinly-sliced corned beef

2 (6 oz.) pkg. Swiss cheese slices, each slice cut into 2" squares

Preparation

- Arrange bread slices on baking sheet. Toast bread on one side.
- Preheat oven in Convection Bake to 375°F (*350°F).
- Spread each slice with 3/4 teaspoon Thousand Island dressing.
- Add small amount of sauerkraut and corned beef to each slice.
- Top each with 1 square Swiss cheese.
- Convection Bake for 5 to 8 minutes or until cheese melts and edges are lightly browned.

SPICY CHICKEN WINGS

Ingredients
DIP

1/2 cup sour cream

2 tablespoons finely chopped red onion

1 clove crushed garlic

1/4 cup minced fresh parsley

1 cup mayonnaise

1/4 cup crumbled bleu cheese

1 tablespoon lemon juice

1/4 teaspoon seasoned salt

1/4 teaspoon freshly ground black pepper

1/8 teaspoon cayenne pepper

CHICKEN WINGS

1/2 cup melted butter

1 teaspoon hot sauce

1/4 teaspoon salt

20 chicken wings, separated into 2 pieces

Preparation
DIP

- Preheat oven in Convection Bake to 400°F (*375°F).
- Combine sour cream, onion, garlic, parsley, mayonnaise, bleu cheese, lemon juice, seasoned salt, pepper and cayenne pepper. Mix well, refrigerate.

CHICKEN WINGS

- Combine melted butter, hot sauce and salt.
- Place chicken wings in 10" x 15" x 1" jelly roll pan. Brush wings with butter mixture.
- Convection Bake for 20 to 25 minutes or until golden brown.
- Serve with dip.

Note: Enter this temperature if your oven does not reduce the oven convection temperature automatically by 25°F in the display.

Wrap dough over cheese to completely enclose. Moisten edges with water to seal.

Gently press braid around side and press ends to seal.

Ingredients

- **1 sheet (half of a 17 oz. pkg.) thawed and unfolded puff pastry**
- **1 (14 to 18 oz.) round of Brie cheese**
- **1 beaten egg**

Preparation

- Preheat oven in Convection Bake to 375°F (*350°F).
- Roll pastry to form a 12-inch square. Cut a 1-inch strip from each side of square. Roll 3 of the strips to 18-inch length and braid or twist to make 1 strip.
- Place Brie, top down, in center of square of dough. Wrap dough over cheese, completely enclosing cheese. Moisten edges of dough with water and seal well.
- Place sealed-side down on baking sheet. Moisten bottom side of dough and gently press braid around side; press ends together to seal.
- Use remaining strip of dough to make decorative cutouts for top. Using a pastry brush, brush egg over dough.
- Convection Bake for 15 to 20 minutes or until pastry is puffed and lightly browned. Let stand 20 minutes before serving.

BAKED BRIE AND BRANDIED MUSHROOMS

Ingredients

- **1 tablespoon margarine or butter**
- **2 tablespoons slivered almonds**
- **1 cup chopped mushrooms**
- **2 minced garlic cloves**
- **1 tablespoon brandy**
- **1 teaspoon chopped fresh tarragon or 1/4 teaspoon dried tarragon leaves**
- **1/8 teaspoon pepper**
- **1 (8 oz.) round Brie cheese**
- **2 sprigs fresh tarragon, optional**

Preparation

- Preheat oven in Convection Bake to 375°F (*350°F).
- Melt margarine in medium skillet over medium heat. Add almonds and stir 2 to 3 minutes or until almonds are browned. Stir in mushrooms, garlic, brandy, tarragon and pepper. Stir 1 to 2 minutes or until mushrooms are tender. Remove from heat.
- Place cheese in ungreased decorative shallow baking dish or 8- or 9-inch pie pan. Spoon mushrooms over top.
- Convection Bake for 10 to 12 minutes or until cheese is soft. Garnish with tarragon sprigs. Serve as a dip or spread with melba toast rounds or crackers.

Reprinted with permission of Pillsbury Company. Adapted by General Electric for convection ovens.

Note: *Enter this temperature if your oven does not reduce the oven convection temperature automatically by 25°F in the display.*

PARMESAN SPINACH ROLL-UPS

PARMESAN SPINACH ROLL-UPS

Ingredients

- **1 egg**
- **2 (10.6 oz.) pkg. Pillsbury® Refrigerated Parmesan Breadsticks**
- **1 (1 lb.) pkg. thawed Green Giant® Frozen Cut Leaf Spinach, squeezed to drain**
- **2 oz. (¹/₂ cup) shredded mozzarella cheese**
- **1 teaspoon lemon juice**
- **1 tablespoon Pillsbury BEST® All Purpose or Unbleached Flour**

Preparation

- Preheat oven in Convection Bake to 375°F (*350°F).
- Lightly grease cookie sheets or use ungreased baking stone.
- Combine egg and contents of both containers of Parmesan spread from breadsticks. Beat well with wire whisk. Add spinach, cheese and lemon juice. Mix well.
- Sprinkle work surface with flour. Unroll dough onto floured surface. Separate into 20 breadsticks. Press or roll each breadstick to form 7 x 1¹/₂-inch strip.
- Spread each strip with 1 tablespoon spinach mixture. Roll up, starting at shortest end. Pinch end of dough to seal. Place rolls, cut side up, 3 inches apart on lightly greased cookie sheets.
- Convection Bake for 10 to 20 minutes or until golden brown. Serve warm.

Reprinted with permission of Pillsbury Company. Adapted by General Electric for convection ovens.

Cooking Tip

To quickly thaw spinach, place in colander or strainer; rinse with warm water until thawed. Squeeze dry with paper towels.

*Note: Enter this temperature if your oven does not reduce the oven convection temperature automatically by 25°F in the display.

APPETIZERS **15**

Green Chile and Cheese Half Moons

Ingredients

- 4 oz. (1 cup) finely shredded Muenster or Monterey Jack cheese
- 2 tablespoons finely chopped green onion tops
- 2 tablespoons finely chopped fresh cilantro or parsley
  Dash salt
- 1 (4.5 oz.) can Old El Paso® Chopped Green Chilies, drained
- 1 (1 lb. 1.3 oz.) can Pillsbury® Grands!® Refrigerated Golden Corn Biscuits or 1 (1 lb. 0.3 oz.) can Pillsbury® Grands!® Refrigerated Buttermilk Biscuits

Preparation

- Preheat oven in Convection Bake to 375°F (*350°F).
- Spray large cookie sheet with nonstick cooking spray.
- Combine cheese, onions, cilantro, salt and green chilies. Mix well.
- Separate dough into 8 biscuits. With serrated knife, cut each biscuit in half horizontally to make 16 rounds. Press or roll each to form a 3½-inch round.
- Place 1 tablespoon cheese mixture in center of each round. Moisten edges of dough. Fold dough over filling. Press edges with fork to seal. Form each filled biscuit into crescent shape. Place on sprayed cookie sheet.
- Convection Bake for 11 to 16 minutes or until golden brown.
- With toothpick, make face to resemble moon on each crescent. Cool 5 minutes. Serve warm.

Reprinted with permission of Pillsbury Company. Adapted by General Electric for convection ovens.

Mini-Parmesan Scones

Ingredients

- 2 tablespoons butter
- ½ cup milk or buttermilk
- 2 cups self-rising flour
- ½ cup freshly grated Parmesan cheese
- 1 teaspoon crushed red pepper flakes
- ½ cup water
  Ground cayenne pepper, optional

Preparation

- Preheat oven in Convection Bake to 375°F (*350°F).
- Melt butter and combine with milk.
- Combine flour, cheese and pepper flakes.
- Make a well in center of flour mixture and add butter mixture. Mix well. Add water, a little at a time, until dough pulls together. Knead dough on lightly floured surface until smooth.
- Divide dough into 2 balls. Press each ball into a circle ¾-inch thick. Cut each circle into 8 wedges and place wedges apart on lightly greased aluminum baking sheet. Sprinkle with ground cayenne pepper if desired.
- Convection Bake for 10 to 15 minutes or until lightly browned.

Cooking Tip

Try adding other savory spices such as lemon peel or onion flakes.

Note: Enter this temperature if your oven does not reduce the oven convection temperature automatically by 25°F in the display.

COCKTAIL MEATBALLS

Ingredients

MEATBALLS
- 1 lb. lean ground beef
- 1/2 cup finely chopped onion
- 1/4 cup dry bread crumbs
- 1 beaten egg
- 2 tablespoons milk
- 2 teaspoons prepared horseradish
- 1/2 teaspoon salt
- 1/8 teaspoon pepper

SAUCE
- 1 cup chili sauce
- 1/4 cup seedless raspberry jam
- 1/4 teaspoon allspice
- 1/4 teaspoon hot pepper sauce

Preparation

MEATBALLS
- Preheat oven in Convection Bake to 375°F (*350°F).
- In a bowl, combine all ingredients and shape into 1-inch meatballs.
- Convection Bake for 10 to 15 minutes or until done.
- Drain on paper towels, if necessary.
- Serve with sauce.

SAUCE
- Combine sauce ingredients in a 2-cup measuring cup. Microwave on HIGH for 45 seconds to 1 minute or until hot.

Cooking Tip
To make meatballs of uniform size, scoop the meat mixture with a small ice cream scoop.

PARTY QUICHE SQUARES

Ingredients
- 1/2 cup finely chopped onion
- 1/4 cup finely chopped sweet red pepper
- 2 tablespoons butter
- 1 (6 oz.) jar marinated artichoke hearts, drained and chopped
- 1 (16 oz.) can drained and flaked crabmeat
- 4 beaten eggs
- 2 cups shredded sharp cheddar cheese
- 1/4 cup fine dry bread crumbs
- 2 tablespoons minced fresh parsley
- 1/4 teaspoon cayenne pepper
- 1/8 teaspoon thyme

Preparation
- Preheat oven in Convection Bake to 375°F (*350°F).
- Sauté onions and red pepper in butter until tender; cool slightly.
- Combine onion mixture, artichoke hearts, crabmeat, eggs, cheese, bread crumbs, parsley, cayenne pepper and thyme; mix well.
- Spoon into a lightly greased 2-quart baking dish.
- Convection Bake for 20 to 30 minutes or until set.
- Let stand 10 minutes. Cut into 1-inch squares.

*Note: Enter this temperature if your oven does not reduce the oven convection temperature automatically by 25°F in the display.

MEATS

Italian Cheese-Stuffed
Meat Loaf–page 22

Citrus Herb Tenderloin with Roasted Peppers and Onions

Ingredients

TENDERLOIN

1 well trimmed whole beef tenderloin (4 to 5 pounds)

2 large red bell peppers, cut into 1 inch wedges

2 large yellow bell peppers, cut into 1 inch wedges

2 large onions, cut lengthwise into ½ inch wedges

1 teaspoon olive oil

SEASONING

2 tablespoons grated lemon peel

2 tablespoons olive oil

2 teaspoons dried thyme leaves

1½ teaspoons salt

1 teaspoon coarse ground black pepper

Preparation

- Combine seasoning ingredients, reserving 2 teaspoons for vegetables. Press remaining seasoning mixture evenly onto surface of beef roast. Place roast on rack in shallow roasting pan. Insert ovenproof thermometer so tip is centered in thickest part of beef, not resting in fat. Do not add water or cover.

- In medium bowl, combine vegetables, reserved seasoning mixture and 1 teaspoon oil, toss to coat.

- Arrange vegetables in single layer on 15" x 10" x 1" jelly roll pan.

- Convection Roast beef and vegetables at 400°F for 40 to 50 minutes for medium rare, 50 to 60 minutes for medium doneness and until vegetables are tender and lightly browned. When placing the beef and vegetables in the oven, make certain that the vegetables are under the roast.

- Remove roast when meat thermometer registers 135°F for medium rare or 150°F for medium doneness.

- Transfer roast to carving board. Tent loosely with aluminum foil. Let roast stand 15 to 20 minutes (Temperature will continue to rise about 10°F to reach 145°F for medium rare or 160°F for medium). Carve roast into slices.

- Serve with roasted vegetables.

Reprinted with permission of the National Cattlemen's Beef Association and the Cattlemen's Beef Board. Adapted by General Electric for convection ovens.

Leg of Lamb with Mustard Glaze

Ingredients

½ cup Dijon mustard

1 teaspoon basil

¼ teaspoon thyme

¼ teaspoon white pepper

2 tablespoons vegetable oil

2 tablespoons Worcestershire sauce

1 (4 to 5 lb.) leg of lamb

Preparation

- Combine mustard, basil, thyme, pepper, oil and Worcestershire sauce.

- Pierce lamb in several places with fork and place fat side up in shallow baking dish. Spread mustard mixture over lamb and chill 2 hours.

- Place roast on broiler pan grid.

- Convection Roast at 325°F to desired doneness.

- Let stand 10 minutes before carving.

Barbecued Spareribs

Ingredients

2½ to 3 lbs. pork spareribs, cut into 2-rib pieces

1 chopped medium onion

1 chopped medium sweet red pepper

2 cloves minced garlic

½ cup catsup

½ cup firmly packed brown sugar

¼ cup molasses

2 tablespoons lemon juice

1 teaspoon prepared brown mustard

Dash hot sauce

Preparation

• Preheat oven in Convection Bake to 375°F (*350°F).

• Place ribs in 3-quart casserole. Cover.

• Convection Bake for 40 minutes and drain.

• In small mixing bowl, combine onion, red pepper, garlic, catsup, brown sugar, molasses, lemon juice, brown mustard and hot sauce.

• Pour sauce over ribs and continue baking uncovered for 25 to 30 minutes.

Beefeater's Pepper-Crusted Roast

Ingredients

1 tablespoon melted butter

1 tablespoon Worcestershire sauce

1 (4 lb.) beef rib roast

3 tablespoons crushed multi-colored peppercorns

1 tablespoon chopped fresh thyme or 1 teaspoon dried thyme leaves

Preparation

• In small bowl, combine butter and Worcestershire sauce. Mix well.

• Place beef roast in ungreased shallow roasting pan. Brush butter mixture over roast. Press peppercorns into top of beef. Sprinkle with thyme.

• Insert meat thermometer so bulb reaches center of thickest part of meat, but does not rest in fat or on bone.

• Convection Roast uncovered at 325°F for 1½ to 2 hours or until meat thermometer registers 150°F for medium-rare or 160°F. for medium doneness.

• Remove beef roast from oven. Cover with tent of foil. Let stand 10 to 15 minutes before carving.

Cooking Tip

Use the oven meat probe to monitor the roast temperature instead of a meat thermometer.

Reprinted with permission of Pillsbury Company. Adapted by General Electric for convection ovens.

Note: Enter this temperature if your oven does not reduce the oven convection temperature automatically by 25°F in the display.

Veal Parmigiana

Ingredients

- 2 (8 oz.) cans tomato sauce
- 1 teaspoon sugar
- 1/2 teaspoon garlic salt
- 1/4 teaspoon oregano
- 1/8 teaspoon pepper
- 2 beaten eggs
- 1 teaspoon salt
- 1/4 teaspoon pepper
- 1 1/2 cups fine dry bread crumbs
- 6 boneless veal cutlets, 1/2 inch thick
- 1/4 cup olive oil
- 1 cup shredded mozzarella cheese
- 1/3 cup grated Parmesan cheese

Preparation

- Preheat oven in Convection Bake to 350°F (*325°F).
- Combine tomato sauce, sugar, garlic salt, oregano and pepper, mix well. Set aside.
- In shallow dish, combine eggs, salt and pepper. Dip veal cutlets in egg mixture and dredge in crumbs.
- Brown cutlets on both sides in hot oil and place in 2-quart (7" x 11") baking dish. Pour tomato sauce over cutlets.
- Convection Bake for 15 to 20 minutes. Sprinkle with mozzarella and Parmesan cheese. Continue baking 5 minutes or until cheese melts.

Apple-Stuffed Pork Chops

Ingredients

- 1 cup herb-seasoned stuffing mix
- 1 cup diced apple
- 1/4 cup finely chopped onion
- 3 tablespoons raisins
- 1/2 cup orange juice
- 2 tablespoons melted butter
- 1 tablespoon grated orange rind
- 1/2 teaspoon salt
- 1/4 teaspoon cinnamon
- 1/4 teaspoon allspice
- 1/8 teaspoon pepper
- 4 1-inch thick center cut pork chops
- 1/2 cup currant jelly
- 2 tablespoons orange juice

Preparation

- Preheat oven in Convection Bake single to 375°F (*350°F).
- In mixing bowl, combine stuffing mix, apple, onion, raisins, 1/2 cup orange juice, butter, orange rind, salt, cinnamon, allspice and pepper.
- Cut a pocket in each pork chop. Divide stuffing evenly among chops.
- Arrange chops in 3-quart (9" x 13") baking dish.
- Combine currant jelly and 2 tablespoons orange juice in glass measure. Microwave at HIGH 1 to 2 minutes. Stir well. Brush half of mixture over chops.
- Convection Bake for 45 to 50 minutes or until tender.
- Spoon remaining jelly mixture over chops before serving.

*Note: Enter this temperature if your oven does not reduce the oven convection temperature automatically by 25°F in the display.

Italian Cheese-Stuffed Meat Loaf

Ingredients

1½ lb. lean ground beef

2 cups soft French bread crumbs

½ cup shredded fresh Parmesan cheese

¼ cup chopped fresh basil or 1½ teaspoons dried basil leaves

2 eggs

4 cloves minced garlic

½ teaspoon salt

¼ teaspoon pepper

1 (8 oz.) can pizza sauce

1½ cups shredded provolone cheese

1 (7.25 oz.) jar drained and chopped roasted red bell peppers

¼ cup chopped ripe olives

Preparation

• Preheat oven in Convection Bake to 375°F (*350°F).

• Spray a 9" x 5" loaf pan with nonstick cooking spray. Set aside.

• In large bowl, combine ground beef, bread crumbs, Parmesan cheese, basil, eggs, garlic, salt, pepper and ½ cup of the pizza sauce. Mix well.

• On large piece of foil, shape the ground beef mixture into 12" x 10" rectangle. Top with provolone cheese, roasted pepper and olives, distributing evenly up to ½-inch of edges. Starting from 10-inch side, roll up jellyroll fashion. Seal edges well. Transfer and place, seam side down, in foil-lined loaf pan.

• Convection Bake for 50 minutes.

• Top with remaining pizza sauce and bake an additional 10 minutes or until loaf is thoroughly cooked in center and meat thermometer registers 160°F.

• Let stand 10 minutes before serving.

Variation

Layered Meatloaf
In loaf pan, place ⅓ of meat mixture and press evenly. Top with ½ of provolone cheese, roasted peppers and olives. Repeat with ⅓ of meat mixture. Repeat cheese, pepper and olive layer. End with last ⅓ of meat mixture.

Cooking Tip

Use the oven meat probe to monitor the meat temperature instead of a meat thermometer.

Reprinted with permission of Pillsbury Company. Adapted by General Electric for convection ovens.

Lemon Pork Chops

MAKES 4 SERVINGS

Ingredients

4 ¾-inch thick center cut pork chops

½ teaspoon salt

¼ teaspoon pepper

⅛ teaspoon thyme

4 onion slices

4 lemon slices

½ cup chili sauce

1 tablespoon brown sugar

Preparation

• Preheat oven in Convection Bake to 375°F (*350°F).

• Arrange chops in 3-quart casserole.

• Combine salt, pepper and thyme and sprinkle over chops. Combine chili sauce and brown sugar; pour over chops. Place onion and lemon slice on each chop.

• Convection Bake for 35 to 40 minutes or until done.

Note: Enter this temperature if your oven does not reduce the oven convection temperature automatically by 25°F in the display.

STUFFED PEPPERS

Ingredients

- 6 medium yellow, green or red peppers
- 1½ lbs. ground chuck
- ½ cup chopped onion
- ½ cup diced celery
- 1 clove minced garlic
- 1 teaspoon salt
- ¼ teaspoon pepper
- ⅛ teaspoon nutmeg
- 1½ cup cooked long grain rice
- 1 (2 oz.) jar drained sliced pimiento
- 1 (15 oz.) can tomato sauce
- 2 tablespoons brown sugar
- 1 tablespoon lemon juice
- 1 tablespoon Worcestershire sauce
- ½ teaspoon garlic salt
- ½ teaspoon basil
- 1½ cup shredded sharp cheddar cheese, optional

Preparation

- Preheat oven in Convection Bake to 375°F (*350°F).
- Cut off tops of peppers. Remove seeds and membrane.
- Cook beef, onion, celery, garlic, salt, pepper and nutmeg until beef is browned. Add rice and pimiento. Mix well.
- Combine tomato sauce, brown sugar, lemon juice, Worcestershire sauce, garlic salt and basil. Pour ¾ of the sauce into the meat mixture. Fill each pepper with about 1¼ cup of filling.
- Arrange stuffed peppers in a 3-quart (9" x 13") baking dish.
- Convection Bake for 30 to 40 minutes until peppers are tender.
- Top with remaining sauce and cheese. Convection Bake an additional 5 minutes or until cheese is melted.

GLAZED PORK ROAST WITH PINEAPPLE SALSA

Ingredients

SALSA

- 2 cups finely chopped fresh pineapple
- 1/2 cup finely chopped sweet red pepper
- 1/2 cup finely chopped green pepper
- 1/4 cup finely chopped red onion
- 2 tablespoons snipped fresh parsley
- 2 teaspoons lemon juice
- 1/2 teaspoon dried red pepper

ROAST

- 1 (2 to 2 1/2 lb.) boneless pork loin roast

GLAZE

- 1/4 cup pineapple preserves
- 1 teaspoon orange juice
- 1/4 teaspoon cinnamon
- 1/8 teaspoon ginger

Preparation

SALSA

- Combine pineapple, red pepper, green pepper, onion, parsley, lemon juice and dried red pepper. Cover and refrigerate.

ROAST

- Place roast on trivet in broiler pan.
- Set oven to Convection Roast 325°. Cook approximately 1 1/2 hours or until meat thermometer inserted in center registers 160°. Brush with Pineapple Glaze during last 10 minutes of cooking time. Remove from oven and let stand for 10 minutes. Serve with Pineapple Salsa.

GLAZE

- Combine pineapple preserves, orange juice, cinnamon and ginger. Blend well.

Cooking Tip

Use the oven meat probe to monitor the pork roast temperature instead of a meat thermometer.

ROSEMARY ROASTED PORK TENDERLOIN

Ingredients

- 1 (1 1/2 to 2 lb.) pork tenderloin
- 3 teaspoons olive or vegetable oil
- 1 tablespoon chopped fresh rosemary or 1 teaspoon dried rosemary leaves
- 1 large clove minced garlic
- 1/8 teaspoon salt
- 1/4 teaspoon coarse ground black pepper

Preparation

- Place pork in ungreased shallow baking pan.
- In small cup, combine oil, rosemary and garlic. Mix well. Brush rosemary mixture over pork. Sprinkle with salt and pepper.
- Convection Roast at 400°F for 35 to 45 minutes or until pork is no longer pink in center.
- Let stand 10 minutes before cutting into slices.

Reprinted with permission of Pillsbury Company. Adapted by General Electric for convection ovens.

Baked Ham with Apple-Mustard Glaze

Ingredients

- 1 (4 to 5 lb.) fully cooked boneless ham
- 1 (10 oz.) jar apple jelly
- 1/4 cup Dijon mustard
- 1 tablespoons brown sugar
- 1/2 teaspoon ginger
- 1 1/2 teaspoons dry mustard

Preparation

- Preheat oven in Convection Bake to 350°F (*325°F).
- Spray shallow roasting pan with nonstick cooking spray and place ham in pan.
- With knife, score ham by cutting diamond shapes about 1/4-inch deep through surface. Cover with foil.
- Convection Bake for 1 hour.
- Meanwhile, in small saucepan, combine apple jelly, Dijon mustard, brown sugar, ginger and dry mustard. Cook over low heat until jelly is melted and mixture is well blended, stirring constantly.
- Remove ham from oven. Brush with about half of the glaze. Cover and return to oven. Bake an additional hour or until thoroughly heated, basting with remaining glaze once or twice.

Reprinted with permission of Pillsbury Company. Adapted by General Electric for convection ovens.

Sherried Peach Pork Chops

Ingredients

- 1 (16 oz.) can peach halves
- 1/4 cup dry sherry
- 1/2 teaspoon coriander
- 1/4 teaspoon cumin
- 1/4 teaspoon ginger
- 1/8 teaspoon cayenne pepper
- 1/8 teaspoon garlic powder
- 4 1-inch thick loin pork chops
- 1/3 cup coarsely chopped chutney

Preparation

- Drain peaches, reserving syrup and set aside.
- Combine reserved syrup, sherry, coriander, cumin, ginger, cayenne pepper and garlic powder; blend well.
- Pierce pork chops with fork and place in a shallow cooking dish. Pour marinade over chops. Let stand 1 hour in refrigerator, turning over once.
- Remove chops from marinade. Discard marinade. Place chops on lightly greased rack of broiling pan.
- Broil on HI BROIL setting 6 inches from heat for 15 to 20 minutes or until lightly browned. Turn chops over and continue broiling 5 to 10 minutes or until desired doneness.
- Fill peach halves with chutney and arrange around chops.
- Continue broiling 3 minutes.

Marinating Tip

Instead of using a covered dish, place pork chops and marinade in a large, self-sealing plastic bag.

Note: Enter this temperature if your oven does not reduce the oven convection temperature automatically by 25°F in the display.

STUFFED CABBAGE LEAVES

Cooked cabbage leaves should be soft and pliable.

Wrap leaf around meat mixture and secure with toothpick.

Ingredients

- **12 large cabbage leaves**
- **1½ lbs. ground chuck**
- **½ cup chopped onion**
- **½ cup diced celery**
- **1 clove minced garlic**
- **1 teaspoon salt**
- **¼ teaspoon pepper**
- **⅛ teaspoon nutmeg**
- **1½ cups cooked long grain rice**
- **1 (2 oz.) jar sliced pimento, drained**
- **1 (15 oz.) can tomato sauce**
- **2 tablespoons brown sugar**
- **1 tablespoon lemon juice**
- **1 tablespoon Worcestershire sauce**
- **½ teaspoon garlic salt**
- **½ teaspoon basil**
- **Toothpicks**
- **1½ cup shredded sharp cheddar cheese, optional**

Preparation

- Preheat oven in Convection Bake to 375°F (*350°F).
- Cook cabbage leaves in boiling water for 5 minutes. Drain and set aside.
- Cook beef, onion, celery, garlic, salt, pepper and nutmeg until beef is browned. Add rice and pimiento. Mix well.
- Combine tomato sauce, brown sugar, lemon juice. Worcestershire sauce, garlic salt and basil. Pour $3/4$ of the sauce into the meat mixture. Divide filling equally onto cabbage leaves. Roll leaves up around filling and secure with toothpicks.
- Arrange cabbage rolls in an ungreased 3-quart (9" x 13") baking dish. Pour remaining sauce over cabbage rolls.
- Convection Bake for 30 to 40 minutes or until thoroughly heated.
- Baste with sauce and top with cheese. Convection Bake an additional 5 minutes or until cheese is melted.

***Note:** Enter this temperature if your oven does not reduce the oven convection temperature automatically by 25°F in the display.*

HERB CRUSTED BEEF RIB ROAST

MAKES 8 TO 10 SERVINGS

Ingredients

ROAST

- 1 (6 to 8 pound) beef rib roast (2 to 4 ribs) small end, chine (back) bone
- 2 tablespoons minced fresh parsley
- 1 tablespoon crushed dried thyme leaves
- 1 tablespoon vegetable oil
- 2 teaspoons cracked black pepper
- 4 cloves garlic

CREAMY HORSERADISH AND CHIVE SAUCE

- 2 cups sour cream
- 1/2 cup prepared horseradish
- 1/3 cup milk
- 2 tablespoons snipped fresh chives
- 1/2 teaspoon ground white pepper

Preparation

ROAST

- Prepare Creamy Horseradish & Chive Sauce the day before.
- In small bowl, combine parsley, thyme, oil, pepper and garlic. Press evenly onto surface of beef roast.
- Place roast, fat side up, in shallow roasting pan. Insert ovenproof meat thermometer so tip is centered in thickest part of meat, not resting in fat or touching bone.
- Convection Roast at 325°F for 2 to 2 1/4 hours for medium rare or 2 1/2 to 2 3/4 hours for medium doneness. Remove roast when meat thermometer registers 135° for medium rare or 150° for medium doneness.
- Transfer roast to carving board. Tent loosely with aluminum foil. Let stand 15 minutes (Temperature will continue to rise approximately 10°F). Carve roast.
- Serve with horseradish sauce.

CREAMY HORSERADISH AND CHIVE SAUCE

- In 1-quart bowl, combine all sauce ingredients. Mix well.
- Cover and refrigerator sauce until ready to serve. Makes approximately 2 3/4 cups.

Reprinted with permission of the National Cattlemen's Beef Association and the Cattlemen's Beef Board. Adapted by General Electric for convection ovens.

LAMB CHOPS WITH CUCUMBER-DILL SAUCE

MAKES 4 TO 6 SERVINGS

Ingredients

CUCUMBER DILL SAUCE

- 1/2 cup mayonnaise
- 1/2 cup sour cream
- 1/2 cup peeled, finely chopped cucumber
- 1 tablespoon lemon juice
- 2 teaspoons dill weed
- 1/2 teaspoon salt

LAMB CHOPS

- 6 loin lamb chops, cut 1 1/2 inches thick

Preparation

CUCUMBER DILL SAUCE

- In small bowl combine mayonnaise, sour cream, cucumber, lemon juice, dill weed and salt. Blend well and set aside.

LAMB CHOPS

- Arrange lamb chops on broiler pan grid and place in oven.
- Convection Roast at 400°F until lightly browned. Turn chops over. Roast until desired doneness.
- Serve with Cucumber Dill Sauce.

Note: Enter this temperature if your oven does not reduce the oven convection temperature automatically by 25°F in the display.

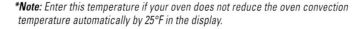

POULTRY

Cornish Hens with Apple Raisin Stuffing—page 36

Mint-Laced Chicken

MAKES 4 TO 6 SERVINGS

Ingredients

- 1 (2½ to 3 lb.) whole chicken
- ½ teaspoon salt
- ¼ teaspoon garlic powder
- ¼ teaspoon lemon pepper
- 1 cup fresh mint leaves
- ¼ cup melted butter
- 1 tablespoon lemon juice

Preparation

- Rinse chicken with cold water and pat dry. Combine salt, garlic powder and lemon pepper. Sprinkle inside chicken cavity, then place mint leaves inside cavity.
- Combine butter and lemon juice. Brush over outside of chicken. Place chicken on broiler pan roasting rack.
- Convection Roast at 325°F for 1 to 1½ hours until done.

Place fresh mint leaves in cavity of chicken.

CRESCENT-WRAPPED CURRIED CHICKEN BREASTS

Press crescent roll perforations together to seal.

Top with chicken and 1/3 cup spinach mixture.

Fold dough over chicken to form a triangle and seal edges.

Ingredients

CHICKEN

- 2 cups water
- 6 (5 to 6 oz.) boneless, skinless chicken breasts
- 1 tablespoon curry powder
- 1 (10 oz.) pkg. frozen chopped spinach, thawed and drained
- 1 (8 oz.) container sour cream
- 1 (3 oz.) pkg. cream cheese
- 1 teaspoon coriander
- 3 (8 oz.) pkgs. crescent rolls
- 1 cup shredded Swiss cheese, divided

BUTTER SAUCE

- 1/2 cup butter
- 1 tablespoon lemon juice
- 1/4 teaspoon pepper
- 1/4 teaspoon dry mustard
- 3 beaten egg yolks

Preparation

CHICKEN

- Preheat oven in Convection Bake to 375°F (*350°F).
- Combine water, chicken and curry. Microwave at MEDIUM HIGH (7) 8 to 10 minutes. Stir after 5 minutes. Drain and set aside.
- Combine spinach, sour cream, cream cheese and coriander. Mix well and set aside.
- Divide each package of crescent rolls in half. Press perforations together to seal. On each square place 1/6 cup Swiss cheese, one chicken breast and about 1/3 cup spinach mixture. Fold dough in half over chicken to form triangles; press edges to seal. Place on ungreased baking sheets.
- Convection Bake for 20 to 25 minutes or until golden brown.

BUTTER SAUCE

- In 2-cup glass measure, place butter, lemon juice, pepper and mustard.
- Microwave on HIGH for 1 minute until butter melts.
- With a wire whisk, blend in egg yolks.
- Microwave on MEDIUM for 30 seconds to 1 minute.
- Pour over cooked chicken.

CHICKEN WITH SPICY CHEDDAR SAUCE

Ingredients

CHICKEN

- 2 cups cornflake crumbs
- 1 teaspoon paprika
- 1/2 teaspoon garlic powder
- 4 boneless chicken breasts

CHEDDAR SAUCE

- 1/2 cup cheese spread with jalapeno peppers
- 1/4 cup sliced pitted ripe olives
- 1 (2 oz.) jar sliced pimento, drained

Preparation

CHICKEN

- Preheat oven in Convection Bake to 375°F (*350°F).
- In mixing bowl, combine cornflake crumbs, paprika and garlic powder. Rinse chicken in water, then coat with crumb mixture. Place chicken in 3-quart (9" x 13") baking dish.
- Convection Bake for 40 to 45 minutes or until done.

CHEDDAR SAUCE

- In 2-cup glass measure, combine cheese spread, olives and pimiento.
- Microwave on HIGH for 1 minute until heated through.
- Pour sauce over cooked chicken.

*Note: Enter this temperature if your oven does not reduce the oven convection temperature automatically by 25°F in the display.

CHICKEN ITALIANO

Ingredients

- ½ lb. sliced fresh mushrooms
- ½ cup chopped onion
- 2 cloves minced garlic
- 2 tablespoons olive oil
- 6 (5 to 6 oz.) boneless skinless chicken breasts
- 1 cup spaghetti sauce
- ⅔ cup dry white wine
- ¾ teaspoon Italian seasoning
- ¼ teaspoon basil
- ¼ cup grated Parmesan cheese
- ½ teaspoon red pepper flakes

Preparation

- Preheat oven in Convection Bake 375°F (*350°F).
- In large skillet, sauté mushrooms, onion and garlic in oil until tender. Add chicken. Sauté until chicken is lightly browned on both sides. Transfer chicken and vegetables to 3-quart (9" x 13") baking dish.
- Combine spaghetti sauce, wine, Italian seasoning and basil. Pour over chicken. Sprinkle with Parmesan cheese and red pepper flakes.
- Convection Bake for 25 to 30 minutes until done.

CHICKEN A LA ROMA

Ingredients

- ¾ cup thinly sliced green onion
- 2 cloves minced garlic
- ½ lb. sliced fresh mushrooms
- 2 tablespoons olive oil
- 1 (8 oz.) can tomato sauce
- ½ cup dry white wine
- ½ cup sliced ripe olives, drained
- 1 tablespoon instant chicken bouillon granules
- 2 teaspoons parsley flakes
- 1 teaspoon basil
- 1 teaspoon oregano
- ½ teaspoon salt
- ¼ teaspoon pepper
- 6 (5 to 6 oz.) boneless, skinless chicken breasts
- 1 (6 oz.) jar marinated artichoke hearts, drained and chopped
- ¼ cup grated Parmesan cheese

Preparation

- Preheat oven in Convection Bake to 400°F (*375°F).
- Sauté onion, garlic and mushrooms in oil until tender. Combine tomato sauce, white wine, olives, bouillon, parsley, basil, oregano, salt and pepper. Add onion mixture. Blend well.
- Place chicken pieces in 3-quart (9" x 13") baking dish. Add tomato mixture.
- Convection Bake for 20-25 minutes.
- Top chicken with chopped artichoke hearts and Parmesan cheese. Continue baking for 10 to 15 minutes or until done.

*Note: Enter this temperature if your oven does not reduce the oven convection temperature automatically by 25°F in the display.

Ingredients

- 1/2 lb. bulk pork sausage
- 1/2 cup chopped onion
- 1/2 cup chopped celery
- 8 cups (about 14 oz.) unseasoned stuffing cubes
- 2 tablespoons finely chopped fresh parsley
- 2 teaspoons poultry seasoning
- 1 teaspoon salt
- 1/4 teaspoon pepper
- 1/4 cup melted margarine or butter
- 2 cups chopped peeled apples
- 2/3 cup raisins
- 2 cups chicken broth or water
- 1 (10 to 12-lb.) whole turkey

Preparation

- In small skillet, brown pork sausage with onion and celery; do not drain.
- Combine stuffing cubes, parsley, poultry seasoning, salt, pepper and margarine. Mix well. Add apples, raisins, broth and sausage mixture with drippings. Mix well.
- Remove and discard neck and giblets from turkey. Rinse turkey inside and out with cold water. Pat dry with paper towels. Spoon stuffing loosely into neck and body cavities of turkey. Do not pack tightly. Set aside remaining stuffing. Turn wings back and tuck tips over shoulder joints. Refasten drumsticks with metal piece or tuck under skin at tail. Fasten neck skin to back with skewers.
- Place stuffed turkey, breast side up, on broiling pan roasting rack. Insert meat thermometer so bulb reaches center of thickest part of thigh but does not rest on bone.
- Place in a cold oven and Convection Roast at 325°F for 2 1/2 to 3 hours or until meat thermometer registers 180°F, stuffing temperature reaches 165°F and leg joint moves easily. Baste with pan juices several times during roasting.
- While turkey is roasting, mix remaining stuffing with additional chicken broth or water to moisten.
- Spoon into slow cooker.
- Cover. Cook on HIGH setting for 30 minutes.
- Reduce setting to LOW. Cook until serving time.
- Mix lightly before serving.

Reprinted with permission of Pillsbury Company. Adapted by General Electric for convection ovens.

Cooking Tip

Use the oven meat probe to monitor the turkey temperature instead of a meat thermometer.

Roast Duck with Orange Sauce MAKES 6 SERVINGS

Ingredients

- 1 (4 to 5 lb.) duck
- ½ cup melted butter
- 2 tablespoons cider vinegar
- 2 tablespoons sugar
- 1 cup chicken broth
- ½ cup orange juice
- 1 tablespoon grated orange peel
- 1 teaspoon lemon juice
- 2 tablespoons cornstarch

Preparation

- Tuck wing tips under back of duck. Brush with melted butter. Place breast side up on broiler pan roasting rack. Set aside.
- In sauce pan, combine vinegar and sugar. Cook until lightly browned. Add broth, orange juice, orange peel, lemon juice and cornstarch. Cook and stir until thickened and smooth. Baste duck with orange sauce.
- Convection Roast at 325°F for 1¾ to 2 hours or until meat thermometer registers 180°F.
- Baste with reserved orange sauce frequently during last 15 minutes of baking time.

Cooking Tip

Use the oven meat probe to monitor the duck temperature instead of a meat thermometer.

Lemon-Herb Roasted Chicken MAKES 6 SERVINGS

Ingredients

- 1 (6-lb.) whole roasting chicken
- 1 thinly sliced lemon
- 1 tablespoon chopped fresh Italian parsley or 1 teaspoon dried parsley flakes
- 1 tablespoon chopped fresh sage or 1 teaspoon dried sage leaves
- 1 tablespoon chopped fresh thyme or 1 teaspoon dried thyme leaves
- 2 large sliced garlic cloves
- 2 tablespoons softened butter
- ¼ teaspoon salt
- ¼ teaspoon coarse ground black pepper

Preparation

- Remove and discard neck and giblets from chicken. Rinse chicken with cold water. Pat dry.
- Loosen skin covering chicken breast meat by slipping fingers down from top between skin and breast meat, gently making a pocket. Place 4 lemon slices and 1 teaspoon of parsley in pocket. Place remaining lemon slices, remaining parsley, sage and thyme in cavity of chicken.
- Rub garlic over outside of chicken. Place garlic in cavity. Loosely tie legs together. Place chicken in shallow roasting pan. Rub outside of chicken with butter; sprinkle with salt and pepper. Insert meat thermometer so bulb reaches center of thickest part of thigh, but does not rest on bone. Do not cover or add water.
- Convection Roast at 400°F for 1½ to 2 hours or until chicken is fork-tender, juices run clear and meat thermometer registers 180 to 185°F.
- Let stand 5 to 10 minutes before carving. Remove and discard lemons from inside of chicken.

Reprinted with permission of Pillsbury Company. Adapted by General Electric for convection ovens.

Cooking Tip

Use the oven meat probe to monitor the chicken temperature instead of a meat thermometer.

Ingredients

- 4 **boneless, skinless chicken breast halves**
- 2 **(1 oz.) slices 97% fat-free ham, cut in half**
- ¼ **cup fat-free cream cheese (from 8-oz. container)**
- 1 **oz. (¼ cup) shredded Swiss cheese**
- 1 **egg white**
- ½ **cup Progresso® Italian Style Bread Crumbs**
- **Nonstick cooking spray**
- **Paprika**

Preparation

- Preheat oven in Convection Bake to 375°F (*350°F).
- Spray 2-quart (7" x 11") baking dish with nonstick cooking spray.
- Place 1 chicken breast half, boned side up, between 2 pieces of plastic wrap or waxed paper. Working from center, gently pound chicken with flat side of meat mallet or rolling pin until about 1/4 inch thick; remove wrap. Repeat with remaining chicken breast halves.
- Place 1 half slice ham on each chicken breast half. Spread each with 1 tablespoon cream cheese; sprinkle each with 1 tablespoon Swiss cheese. Starting at short end, roll up. Secure with wooden toothpicks; press edges to seal.
- Place egg white in small shallow bowl; beat slightly. Place breads crumbs in another shallow bowl. Carefully dip chicken rolls in egg white. Coat with bread crumbs.
- Place chicken rolls, seam side down, in sprayed pan.
- Spray tops of each roll with cooking spray.
- Convection Bake for 35 to 45 minutes or until chicken is fork–tender and juices run clear.
- Remove toothpicks before serving. Sprinkle with paprika.

Reprinted with permission of Pillsbury Company. Adapted by General Electric for convection ovens.

CHICKEN ENCHILADAS   MAKES 5 SERVINGS

Ingredients

- 4 **(5 oz.) cans cooked chicken, drained**
- 2 **cups sour cream**
- 1 **(10¾ oz.) can cream of chicken soup**
- 1½ **cups shredded Monterey Jack cheese**
- 1½ **cups shredded Colby cheese**
- 1 **(4 oz.) can chopped green chilies, drained**
- 2 **tablespoons chopped onion**
- ¼ **teaspoon pepper**
- 10 **(8-inch) flour tortillas**
- 1 **cup shredded Colby cheese**

Preparation

- Preheat oven in Convection Bake to 375°F (*350°F).
- In large mixing bowl, combine chicken, sour cream, soup, Monterey Jack cheese, Colby cheese, green chilies, onion and pepper. Mix well.
- Place 1/2 cup of mixture on each tortilla; roll up and place seam side down in 3-quart (9" x 13") baking dish.
- Convection Bake for 15 to 20 minutes.
- Sprinkle with 1 cup Colby cheese and continue baking 5 minutes or until cheese is melted.

Note: Enter this temperature if your oven does not reduce the oven convection temperature automatically by 25°F in the display.

Oven Barbecued Chicken

Ingredients

- 6 (5 to 6 oz.) boneless, skinless chicken breasts
- 1 large sliced onion
- 1/2 cup sliced celery
- 1/4 cup water
- 1/2 teaspoon salt
- 1/8 teaspoon pepper
- 3/4 cup catsup
- 1/4 cup honey
- 1 tablespoon Worcestershire sauce
- 1 tablespoon prepared mustard
- 1 tablespoon cider vinegar
- 1/8 teaspoon allspice

Preparation

- Preheat oven in Convection Bake to 350°F (*325°F).
- Place chicken pieces in 3-quart (9" x 13") baking dish. Arrange onion slices and celery around chicken pieces. Pour water over chicken. Sprinkle with salt and pepper. Cover with foil.
- Convection Bake for 20 to 25 minutes.
- Combine catsup, honey, Worcestershire sauce, mustard, vinegar and allspice. Pour sauce over chicken. Bake an additional 20 to 25 minutes or until done.

Chicken Parmesan

Ingredients

- 4 (5 to 6 oz.) boneless, skinless chicken breasts
- 3/4 cup seasoned dry bread crumbs
- 1/4 cup grated Parmesan cheese
- 1/4 teaspoon paprika
- 1 beaten egg
- 1/4 cup water
- 1 cup spaghetti sauce
- 1 cup shredded mozzarella cheese

Preparation

- Preheat oven in Convection Bake to 400°F (*375°F).
- Pound each chicken breast to about 1/4" thickness. Set aside.
- Combine bread crumbs, Parmesan cheese and paprika. Set aside.
- In shallow dish, blend egg and water. Dip chicken breasts in egg mixture and then in bread crumb mixture.
- In 2-quart (7" x 11") baking dish, arrange breaded chicken. Pour spaghetti sauce over top and sprinkle with mozzarella cheese.
- Convection Bake for 30 to 35 minutes until done.

*Note: Enter this temperature if your oven does not reduce the oven convection temperature automatically by 25°F in the display.

CORNISH HENS WITH
APPLE RAISIN STUFFING

Ingredients

STUFFING

  3 **tablespoons margarine or butter**

½ **cup chopped green onions**

  1 **unpeeled, chopped red baking apple**

  4 **cups unseasoned dry bread cubes**

½ **cup raisins**

¼ **teaspoon salt**

¼ **teaspoon allspice**

¼ **cup apple juice**

CORNISH HENS

  4 **(24 oz.) Cornish game hens**

¼ **teaspoon salt**

⅛ **teaspoon pepper**

¼ **cup apple jelly**

  2 **tablespoons margarine or butter**

Preparation

- Preheat oven in Convection Bake to 375°F (*350°F).
- Melt 3 tablespoons margarine in large skillet. Add onions and apple; cook and stir until tender. Stir in all remaining stuffing ingredients.
- Remove and discard neck and giblets from game hens. Split each game hen in half. Rinse game hens with cold water; pat dry. Sprinkle with salt and pepper.
- Spread stuffing in ungreased 15" x 10" x 1" baking pan. Place game hens, skin side up, over stuffing.
- Melt jelly with 2 tablespoons margarine over low heat. Brush over game hens.
- Convection Bake for 30 to 40 minutes or until game hens are fork-tender and juices run clear.

Reprinted with permission of Pillsbury Company. Adapted by General Electric for convection ovens.

SWEET AND TANGY CHICKEN

Ingredients

  6 **boneless, skinless chicken breasts**

¾ **cup bottled Russian salad dressing**

¾ **cup apricot preserves**

  2 **tablespoons mayonnaise**

  1 **(1¾ oz.) pkg. dry onion soup mix**

Preparation

- Preheat oven in Convection Bake to 375°F (*350°F).
- Arrange chicken in 3-quart (9" x 13") baking dish.
- Combine dressing, preserves, mayonnaise and onion soup mix. Pour over chicken.
- Convection Bake for 25 to 30 minutes or until done.

Note: Enter this temperature if your oven does not reduce the oven convection temperature automatically by 25°F in the display.

Garlic Shrimp–page 41

SCALLOPED OYSTERS

Ingredients

- 1/2 **cup chopped onion**
- 1/2 **cup chopped green pepper**
- 2 **tablespoons butter**
- 1/4 **cup melted butter**
- 2 **cups buttery cracker crumbs**
- 1/2 **teaspoon salt**
- 1/8 **teaspoon pepper**
- 2 **(8 oz.) cans fresh oysters, drained**
- 1 **teaspoon Worcestershire sauce**
- 1 **cup evaporated milk**

Preparation

- Preheat oven in Convection Bake to 375°F (*350°F).
- In skillet, sauté onion and green pepper in 2 tablespoons butter until tender. Set aside.
- Combine 1/4 cup melted butter, cracker crumbs, salt and pepper. Mix well.
- In 2-quart casserole, layer 1/3 crumb mixture, one can of oysters and half of onion and green pepper mixture. Repeat layers.
- Combine Worcestershire sauce and evaporated milk. Pour over casserole. Top with 1/3 crumb mixture.
- Convection Bake for 25 to 35 minutes.

FISH FILLETS ALMONDINE

Ingredients

- 1 **lb. fresh fish fillets**
- 2 **tablespoons melted butter**
- 1/2 **teaspoon lemon pepper**
- 1/4 **teaspoon dill weed**
- 1/4 **teaspoon salt**
- 1/2 **cup toasted slivered almonds**
- 1 **tablespoon chopped fresh parsley**

Preparation

- Preheat oven in Convection Bake to 375°F (*350°F).
- Brush fish on both sides with butter. Sprinkle with lemon pepper, dill weed and salt. Place fish in 2-quart (7" x 11") baking dish.
- Convection Bake for 10 to 15 minutes or until fish flakes easily when tested with a fork. Top with almonds and parsley before serving.

Cooking Tip

Toasting nuts really brings out the flavor. Spread nuts in a single layer on a baking sheet and toast in a 350°F oven for 3 to 5 minutes, or stir in a dry, heavy skillet over low heat for 2 or 3 minutes. Watch closely. Be ready to remove from oven or heat as soon as they start to color.

*__Note:__ Enter this temperature if your oven does not reduce the oven convection temperature automatically by 25°F in the display.

LEMON PEPPER SALMON STEAKS

Ingredients

2 tablespoons melted butter

2 teaspoons lemon juice

6 (5 oz.) salmon steaks

2 teaspoons lemon pepper

1/2 teaspoon garlic powder

1/2 teaspoon tarragon

1/4 teaspoon salt

1/4 teaspoon paprika

6 thin lemon slices, optional

Preparation

• Preheat oven in Convection Roast to 400°F .

• Combine butter and lemon juice. Brush over both sides of salmon.

• Combine lemon pepper, garlic powder, tarragon, salt and paprika. Sprinkle over both sides of salmon.

• Place salmon on broiler pan with grid.

• Convection Roast 8 to 10 minutes until lightly browned on first side. Turn salmon over and top each steak with lemon slice.

• Convection Roast an additional 8 to 10 minutes until fish flakes easily when tested with a fork.

COMPANY LOBSTER TAILS

Ingredients
LOBSTER TAILS

1/4 cup seasoned dry bread crumbs

2 tablespoons minced fresh parsley

1/4 teaspoon onion powder

1/8 teaspoon paprika

1/8 teaspoon salt

4 (8 oz.) thawed lobster tails

1/4 cup melted butter

2 tablespoons lemon juice

LEMON BUTTER

1/2 cup butter

2 tablespoons lemon juice

Preparation
LOBSTER TAILS

• Combine bread crumbs, parsley, onion powder, paprika and salt. Set aside.

• With kitchen shears, cut lobster through center of soft underside of shell to the tail. Loosen lobster from shell with fingers, leaving meat attached to tail section. Place lobster tails on rack of broiler pan. Shield ends of tails with aluminum foil.

• Combine butter and lemon juice. Brush over lobster tails.

• Set oven to Lo Broil setting. Broil 3 inches from heat for 9 minutes. Brush with remaining butter mixture. Broil 8 to 9 minutes longer or until done.

• Sprinkle evenly with crumb mixture. Serve with Lemon Butter.

LEMON BUTTER

• Microwave butter and lemon juice on MEDIUM for 1 to 2 minutes or until butter is melted.

*Note: Enter this temperature if your oven does not reduce the oven convection temperature automatically by 25°F in the display.

TUNA CROQUETTES WITH LEMON SAUCE

Ingredients

TUNA CROQUETTES

1³/₄ cups dry bread crumbs, divided

1 (6¹/₂ oz.) can water-packed tuna, drained

1 cup grated carrots

¹/₂ cup finely chopped celery

¹/₂ cup milk

2 beaten eggs

1 tablespoon finely chopped onion

1 teaspoon lemon juice

¹/₂ teaspoon salt

¹/₄ teaspoon pepper

LEMON SAUCE

1 tablespoon cornstarch

1 cup milk

2 tablespoons melted butter

¹/₈ teaspoon pepper

¹/₃ cup chopped fresh parsley

1 tablespoon lemon juice

Preparation

TUNA CROQUETTES

- Preheat oven in Convection Bake to 375°F (*350°F).
- In large mixing bowl, combine 1 cup dry bread crumbs, tuna, carrots, celery, milk, eggs, onion, lemon juice, salt and pepper. Mix well. Shape mixture into 6 cone-shaped portions. Roll in remaining crumbs to coat all sides. Place croquettes in a 3-quart (9" x 13") baking dish.
- Convection Bake for 25 to 30 minutes or until done. Serve with lemon sauce.

LEMON SAUCE

- Dissolve cornstarch in milk. Add melted butter and pepper.
- Microwave at HIGH for 2 to 3 minutes or until thickened, stirring after 1¹/₂ minutes. Stir in fresh parsley and lemon juice before serving.

SALMON TERRINE

Ingredients

2 (16 oz.) cans drained salmon with bone and skin removed

³/₄ cup dry bread crumbs

¹/₂ cup milk

1 beaten egg

¹/₄ cup melted butter

2 tablespoons grated Parmesan cheese

1 teaspoon dill weed

¹/₂ teaspoon salt

Preparation

- Preheat oven in Convection Bake to 350°F (*325°F).
- In large bowl, combine salmon, bread crumbs, milk, egg, butter, Parmesan cheese, dill weed and salt. Mix well. Pack mixture firmly into a well greased 8" x 4" loaf pan.
- Convection Bake for 35 to 45 minutes or until done. Let stand 5 minutes.

Interesting Fact

Salmon is high in protein and also a rich source of vitamin A, the B-group vitamins and Omega-3 oils. The soft bones in canned salmon are an excellent calcium source.

*Note: Enter this temperature if your oven does not reduce the oven convection temperature automatically by 25°F in the display.

BAKED FISH WITH CHEESE

Ingredients

- 1/2 cup shredded four-cheese blend
- 2 tablespoons sour cream
- 1 lb. fresh sole or cod fillets
- 2 tablespoons melted butter
- 2 teaspoons tarragon
- Salt and pepper to taste

Preparation

- Preheat oven in Convection Bake to 375°F (*350°F).
- Combine shredded cheese and sour cream. Set aside.
- Brush fish on both sides with melted butter. Sprinkle with tarragon, salt and pepper. Place fillets in 3-quart (9" x 13") baking dish.
- Convection Bake for 10 minutes. Top with cheese mixture.
- Convection Bake for and additional 10 to 15 minutes or until fish flakes easily with fork.

SWORDFISH WITH ORANGE SAUCE

Ingredients

ORANGE SAUCE

- 2/3 cup orange marmalade
- 1/3 cup pineapple juice
- 2 teaspoons prepared horseradish
- 1/4 teaspoon garlic powder
- 1/4 teaspoon coriander
- Dash hot sauce

SWORDFISH

- 4 (6 oz.) swordfish steaks
- 3 tablespoons lime juice
- 2 tablespoons melted butter

Preparation

ORANGE SAUCE

- Combine orange marmalade, pineapple juice, horseradish, garlic powder, coriander and hot sauce. Cook over medium low heat for 5 minutes. Set aside and keep warm.

SWORDFISH

- Place swordfish steaks on lightly greased grid of broiler pan.
- Combine lime juice and butter. Brush over steaks.
- Broil at Lo Broil setting 4 inches from heat for 10-15 minutes. Turn fish over and continue broiling 10-15 minutes or until done. Brush occasionally with lime-butter mixture.
- Serve with Orange Sauce.

GARLIC SHRIMP

Ingredients

- 1 lb. peeled and deveined large shrimp
- 3 tablespoons melted butter
- 4 cloves minced garlic
- 1 tablespoon snipped, fresh parsley
- Fresh shredded spinach
- Grated Parmesan cheese

Preparation

- Preheat oven to Convection Roast 450°F.
- Combine shrimp, butter, garlic and parsley. Stir to coat evenly. Spread shrimp in a single layer on a 10" x 15" baking sheet.
- Convection Roast for 4 to 8 minutes or until done.
- Arrange on shredded spinach. Sprinkle with Parmesan cheese.

__Note:__ Enter this temperature if your oven does not reduce the oven convection temperature automatically by 25°F in the display.

Spiced Fish Bake

Ingredients

- 4 (6 oz.) fresh talapia fillets
- 1 tablespoon melted butter
- 1 teaspoon paprika
- 1/2 teaspoon salt
- 1/2 teaspoon lemon pepper
- 1/4 teaspoon dry mustard
- 1/4 teaspoon garlic powder
  Dash ground red pepper

Preparation

- Preheat oven in Convection Bake to 375°F (*350°F).
- Brush fish with melted butter.
- Combine paprika, salt, lemon pepper, dry mustard, garlic powder and red pepper. Sprinkle evenly over fish.
- Place fish in 2-quart (7" x 11") baking dish.
- Convection Bake for 8 to 10 minutes or until fish flakes easily when tested with a fork.

Cooking Tip

The freshest fish makes the most delicious eating. When shopping for fish, remember that fresh fish has very little smell and that the flesh should feel firm and elastic to the touch. Always cook fish as soon as possible after purchasing. Orange roughy fillets may be substituted for talapia fillets if they are not available.

Sole Florentine

Ingredients

- 1/4 cup chopped onion
- 1 clove minced garlic
- 2 teaspoons olive oil
- 1 (10 oz.) pkg. frozen, chopped spinach, thawed and drained
- 1 (2 oz.) jar diced pimiento, drained
- 1/8 cup crumbled Feta cheese
- 1/2 teaspoon grated lemon rind
- 1/2 teaspoon salt
- 1/4 teaspoon oregano
- 1/8 teaspoon white pepper
- 1 lb. fresh sole fillets
- 2 tablespoons melted butter
- 2 teaspoons lemon juice
  Paprika

Preparation

- Preheat oven in Convection Bake to 400°F (*375°F).
- In skillet, sauté onion and garlic in olive oil until tender. Combine onion and garlic mixture, spinach, pimiento, cheese, lemon rind, salt, oregano and pepper. Spread spinach mixture in 8-inch square baking dish.
- Arrange fish over spinach. Combine butter and lemon juice. Brush over fish and sprinkle with paprika.
- Convection Bake for 20 to 25 minutes or until fish flakes easily when tested with a fork.

Cooking Tip

Use the "10-minute rule." Measure the fish at its thickest point. Cook fresh fish 10 minutes per inch if cooked alone (15 minutes if cooked in a sauce). Orange roughy fillets may be substituted for sole fillets if they are not available.

This recipe can easily be doubled and baked in a 3-quart (9" x 13") baking dish.

*Note: Enter this temperature if your oven does not reduce the oven convection temperature automatically by 25°F in the display.

ITALIAN BAKED FISH

Ingredients

- **2** tablespoons olive oil
- **1** tablespoon lemon juice
- **1** cup chopped tomatoes
- **1½** cups sliced fresh mushrooms
- **¼** cup chopped onion
- **¼** cup chopped green pepper
- **2** tablespoons chopped fresh parsley
- **¾** teaspoon oregano
- **½** teaspoon seasoned salt
- **¼** teaspoon garlic powder
- **1** (16 oz.) pkg. frozen cod fillets, thawed
- Dash salt
- Dash pepper

Preparation

- Preheat oven in Convection Bake to 375°F (*350°F).
- In skillet, sauté olive oil, lemon juice, tomatoes, mushrooms, onion, green pepper, parsley, oregano, seasoned salt and garlic powder until onion is tender.
- Place fish fillets in 2-quart (7" x 11") baking dish. Sprinkle with salt and pepper. Spoon vegetable mixture over fillets.
- Convection Bake for 20 to 25 minutes or until fish flakes easily with fork.

BAKED GROUPER WITH CREOLE SAUCE

Ingredients

- **4** (6 oz.) fresh grouper fillets
- **1** (8 oz.) can tomato sauce
- **1** tablespoon dry white wine
- **2** teaspoons sugar
- **1** teaspoon basil
- **½** teaspoon thyme
- **½** teaspoon salt
- **¼** teaspoon oregano
- **¼** teaspoon crushed red pepper
- **¼** cup thinly sliced green onion

Preparation

- Preheat oven in Convection Bake to 425°F (*400°F).
- Place fillets in an 8-inch square baking dish.
- Combine tomato sauce, wine, sugar, basil, thyme, salt, oregano and pepper. Blend well and pour over fish.
- Convection Bake for 20 to 25 minutes or until fish flakes easily when tested with a fork.
- Sprinkle with onions before serving.

Cooking Tip

Orange roughy fillets may be substituted for grouper fillets if they are not available.

This recipe can easily be doubled and baked in a 3-quart (9" x 13") baking dish.

*****Note:** Enter this temperature if your oven does not reduce the oven convection temperature automatically by 25°F in the display.

Spoon 1/3 cup of shrimp mixture onto each tortilla.

Roll up tightly and place seam side down in baking dish.

Ingredients

CHEESE SAUCE

- 1/2 cup chopped sweet red pepper
- 1/2 cup minced onion
- 1/2 cup chopped green pepper
- 1/4 cup butter
- 1/2 teaspoon oregano
- 1/2 teaspoon salt
- 1/4 teaspoon garlic powder
- 1/8 teaspoon black pepper
- 1/8 teaspoon cayenne pepper
- 3/4 cup whipping cream
- 1 tablespoon all-purpose flour
- 3 cups divided, Monterey Jack cheese
- 1/2 cup sour cream

FILLING

- 1/4 cup melted butter
- 1 lb. uncooked, peeled and deveined medium shrimp
- 1 cup peeled and chopped tomatoes
- 1/2 cup chopped onion

TOPPING

- 1 cup peeled and chopped tomatoes
- 8 (9-inch) flour tortillas
- 1/2 cup chopped onion

Preparation

CHEESE SAUCE

- Preheat oven in Convection Bake to 375°F (*350°F).
- In skillet sauté red pepper, onion and green pepper in 1/4 cup butter until crisp-tender. Add oregano, salt, garlic powder, pepper, cayenne pepper, cream and flour. Blend well. Continue cooking 3 minutes or until slightly thickened. Add 1 1/2 cups cheese; stir until melted. Add sour cream. Stir to blend. Set cheese sauce aside.

FILLING

- Microwave 1/4 cup butter, shrimp and 1/2 cup onion at HIGH (10) 4 to 5 minutes. Stir after 2 minutes. Remove shrimp and chop. Return to butter and onion and add 1 cup tomatoes and 1/2 of cheese sauce.
- Spoon 1/3 cup shrimp mixture into each tortilla. Roll up tightly. Arrange, seam side down, in 3-quart (9" x 13") baking dish. Spoon remaining cheese sauce over tortillas.
- Convection Bake for 25 to 35 minutes.

TOPPING

- Sprinkle enchiladas with remaining 1 1/2 cups cheese, 1/2 cup onion and 1 cup tomatoes immediately after removing from oven.

> **Variation**
> Replace the shrimp with chicken.

__Note:__ Enter this temperature if your oven does not reduce the oven convection temperature automatically by 25°F in the display.

Cheesy Tuna
Tater Pie–page 52

CHICKEN-ASPARAGUS CASSEROLE

Ingredients

- 2 (10 oz.) pkgs. frozen asparagus spears, thawed and well drained
- 2 (8 oz.) cans sliced water chestnuts, drained
- 2 cups sliced celery
- 4 cups chopped cooked chicken
- 2 (10¾ oz.) cans cream of chicken soup
- 1 (8 oz.) carton sour cream
- ½ cup dry sherry
- ½ cup milk
- 1 teaspoon salt
- 1 cup chopped toasted almonds
- ½ cup grated Parmesan cheese

Preparation

- Preheat oven in Convection Bake to 375°F (*350°F).
- Layer asparagus, water chestnuts, celery and chicken in a 3-quart (9" x 13") baking dish.
- Combine soup, sour cream, sherry, milk and salt. Mix well and spoon over chicken. Top with chopped almonds and grated cheese.
- Convection Bake for 30 to 40 minutes until bubbly and cheese is lightly browned.

TURKEY-HAM-CHEESE CASSEROLE

Ingredients

- 6 pieces of toasted white bread, cut into 1-inch cubes
- 1½ cups (¼ pound) thin sliced ham, cut into pieces
- 4 cups cubed cooked turkey
- 1 chopped tomato
- 4 pieces cooked and crumbled bacon
- 4 cups cheese sauce

CHEESE SAUCE

- 6 tablespoons butter
- ¼ cup plus 2 tablespoons flour
- ½ teaspoon white pepper
- 3 cups milk
- 2½ cups grated American cheese
- ½ cup grated sharp cheese

Preparation

- Preheat oven in Convection Bake to 400°F (*375°F).
- In a 3-quart (9" x 13") baking dish layer: toast, cheese sauce, ham, cheese sauce, turkey, tomato, cheese sauce, and top with bacon.
- Convection Bake for 15 to 20 minutes.

CHEESE SAUCE

- Melt butter in large pan on low heat. Add flour and pepper stirring well with wire whisk until smooth. Add milk slowly, stirring well. Raise heat setting to medium. Stir sauce slowly as it begins to cook.
- When sauce starts to bubble, stir in grated cheeses. Stir slowly until it starts to thicken.

Cooking Tip

Use leftover turkey from holiday meals and special occasions.

*Note: Enter this temperature if your oven does not reduce the oven convection temperature automatically by 25°F in the display.

TURKEY TETRAZZINI

Ingredients

- 1/4 cup melted butter
- 1/4 cup all-purpose flour
- 1 cup chicken broth
- 1 cup half and half
- 4 cups chopped cooked turkey
- 1 (2 oz.) jar sliced, chopped pimiento
- 1 (7 oz.) package spaghetti, cooked and drained
- 1 (4 oz.) can sliced mushrooms, drained
- 1/2 teaspoon salt
- 1/2 teaspoon pepper
- 1/4 cup grated Parmesan cheese

Preparation

- Preheat oven in Convection Bake to 375°F (*350°F).
- In 4-cup glass measure, combine butter and flour. Gradually add broth and half and half, stirring until smooth. Microwave at MEDIUM HIGH for 5 to 6 minutes or until thickened, stirring every 2 minutes.
- Combine sauce, turkey, pimiento, spaghetti, mushrooms, salt and pepper. Blend well.
- Spoon mixture into 3-quart (9" x 13") baking dish. Sprinkle Parmesan cheese over top.
- Convection Bake for 20 to 25 minutes until heated through.

Variations

This popular casserole can be made with leftover turkey or chicken. For a tasty variation, replace half the turkey with chopped cooked ham.

Serve Turkey Tetrazzini with steamed broccoli and crunchy apple salad. An easy dessert of orange sherbet and ginger-snaps completes the meal.

CRAB-SHRIMP BAKE

Ingredients

- 1 (6 oz.) pkg. cooked long grain and wild rice
- 2 cups buttery cracker crumbs
- 4 tablespoons butter, divided
- 1 cup fresh sliced mushrooms
- 1/2 cup chopped celery
- 1/4 cup finely chopped onion
- 2 (4 1/2 oz.) cans shrimp, drained
- 1 (6 oz.) can crabmeat, drained and flaked
- 1 (10 3/4 oz.) can cream of mushroom soup
- 1 (2 oz.) jar sliced pimiento, drained
- 1 tablespoon lemon juice

Preparation

- Preheat oven in Convection Bake to 375°F (*350°F).
- Cook rice according to package directions.
- Combine cracker crumbs and 2 tablespoons of butter. Set aside.
- Sauté mushrooms, celery and onion in remaining butter for 4 to 5 minutes or until crisp-tender.
- Combine rice, mushroom mixture, shrimp, crabmeat, soup, pimiento and lemon juice. Mix well.
- Spoon mixture into a 2-quart (7" x 11") baking dish. Top with crumb mixture.
- Convection Bake for 25 to 35 minutes or until bubbly.

*Note: Enter this temperature if your oven does not reduce the oven convection temperature automatically by 25°F in the display.

CHILE CON CARNE WITH NOODLES

Wear gloves when chopping hot peppers to protect from burning reaction.

Ingredients

- 1½ lbs. lean ground beef
- ½ cup chopped onion
- ½ cup chopped green pepper
- 1 chopped hot pepper, optional
- 2 cups shredded Cheddar cheese
- 8 oz. egg noodles, cooked and drained
- 1 (15 oz.) can chili beans
- 1 (8 oz.) can tomato sauce
- 1 tablespoon chili powder
- ½ teaspoon cumin
- ½ teaspoon salt
- ¼ teaspoon pepper
- Sliced ripe olives, optional

Preparation

- Preheat oven in Convection Bake to 375°F (*350°F).
- Cook ground beef, onion, green pepper and hot pepper until beef is browned. Drain.
- Combine beef mixture, cheese, noodles, chili beans, tomato sauce, chili powder, cumin, salt and pepper in a 3-quart (9" x 13") baking dish. Mix well.
- Convection Bake for 20 to 30 minutes or until hot.
- Garnish with sliced ripe olives, if desired.

CHICKEN POT PIE

Ingredients

- 4 boneless, skinless chicken breasts
- 1 teaspoon salt
- ½ cup chopped green onion
- ½ cup chopped celery
- ⅓ cup all-purpose flour
- 1 (2 oz) jar sliced pimiento
- 1 (10 oz.) pkg. frozen peas and carrots, thawed
- ½ teaspoon pepper
- ¾ teaspoon thyme
- 1 (14 oz) can chicken broth
- Pastry for 2 (9-inch) pie crusts

Preparation

- Preheat oven in Convection Bake to 425°F (*400°F).
- Cut chicken into ½ inch cubes.
- Combine chicken with the other filling ingredients. Mix well. Pour into a 3-quart (9" x 13") baking dish.
- Top with pie crust, crimping edges of crust around inside of dish. Decorate with pastry cutouts if desired. Cut slits in top of crust to allow steam to escape.
- Convection Bake for 30 to 40 minutes or until golden brown.

Note: Enter this temperature if your oven does not reduce the oven convection temperature automatically by 25°F in the display.

LASAGNA

Ingredients

- 1 lb. ground beef
- 1/2 cup chopped onion
- 2 (8 oz.) cans tomato sauce
- 1 (6 oz.) can tomato paste
- 1/4 cup water
- 1 3/4 teaspoons basil
- 1 1/2 teaspoons oregano
- 1 teaspoon parsley flakes
- 3/4 teaspoon garlic salt
- 1 (12 oz.) carton small curd cottage cheese
- 1 beaten egg
- 1/4 teaspoon seasoned salt
- 6 cooked lasagna noodles
- 2 (6 oz.) pkgs. sliced mozzarella cheese
- 1/2 cup grated Parmesan cheese

Preparation

- Preheat oven in Convection Bake to 400°F (*375°F).
- In skillet over medium high heat, cook beef and onion until meat is browned. Drain. Stir in tomato sauce, tomato paste, water, basil, oregano, parsley flakes and garlic salt. Set meat sauce aside.
- Combine cottage cheese, egg and seasoned salt.
- In 3-quart (9" x 13") baking dish, spread 1/3 of meat sauce over bottom of pan. Top with half of lasagna noodles, then half of the cheese mixture and half of mozzarella cheese. Repeat layers, ending with meat sauce. Sprinkle top with Parmesan cheese.
- Convection Bake for 25 to 30 minutes.

Variations

Substitute 1 (15-oz.) carton ricotta cheese for the cottage cheese for a firmer lasagna.

1 lb. ground sausage may be substituted for the ground beef. A mixture of half sausage/half ground beef may also be used.

CAROLINA BRUNCH-STYLE GRITS

Ingredients

- 1 cup uncooked quick-cooking grits
- 4 cups water
- 1 (11 oz.) can Green Giant® Mexicorn® Whole Kernel Corn, Red and Green Peppers, drained
- 1 (9 oz.) pkg. Green Giant® Frozen Spinach, thawed
- 1 (1.25 oz.) pkg. Old El Paso® Taco Seasoning Mix
- 2 tablespoons chopped onion
- 2 tablespoons margarine or butter
- 8 oz. (2 cups) shredded Cheddar cheese

Preparation

- Preheat oven in Convection Bake to 375°F (*350°F).
- Cook grits in 4 cups water. Use cooking time on package directions.
- Combine cooked grits and all remaining ingredients except 1 cup of the cheese in an ungreased 3-quart (9" x 13") baking dish. Mix well. Sprinkle top with remaining 1 cup cheese.
- Convection Bake for 20 to 30 minutes or until edges are bubbly and cheese is melted.

Cooking Tip

To quickly thaw spinach, cut small slit in center of pouch; microwave on HIGH for 2 to 3 minutes or until thawed. Remove spinach from pouch. Squeeze dry with paper towels.

Reprinted with permission of Pillsbury Company. Adapted by General Electric for convection ovens.

Note: Enter this temperature if your oven does not reduce the oven convection temperature automatically by 25°F in the display.

CHEESY CHICKEN CASSEROLE

Ingredients

- 2-3 boneless, skinless chicken breasts
- 1 cup chopped mushrooms
- 1/2 cup chopped green pepper
- 1/2 cup chopped onion
- 6 tablespoons all-purpose flour
- 8 oz. uncooked egg noodles
- 1 (13³/₄ oz.) can chicken broth
- 1¹/₄ cups milk
- 1/4 cup melted butter
- 1/2 cup water
- ³/₄ teaspoon salt
- 1/4 teaspoon pepper
- 1¹/₂ cups shredded Cheddar cheese

Preparation

- Preheat oven in Convection Bake to 375°F (*350°F).
- Cut chicken into small pieces.
- In large mixing bowl, combine all ingredients except cheese. Mix well. Pour into 3-quart (9" x 13") baking dish. Top with Cheddar cheese. Cover with foil.
- Convection Bake for 30 to 35 minutes. Remove foil and Convection Bake for an additional 10 minutes.

ENCHILADA CASSEROLE

Place 6 tortillas in dish to start first layer.

Sprinkle first layer with cheese and repeat layers.

Ingredients

- 2 lbs. lean ground beef
- 1 chopped medium onion
- 1 (11 oz.) can corn with red and green peppers, drained
- 1 (10 oz.) can hot or mild enchilada sauce
- 1 (8 oz.) can tomato sauce
- 1 (4 oz.) can chopped green chilies, drained
- 1/2 cup picanté sauce
- 1/2 teaspoon oregano
- 1/2 teaspoon salt
- 1/4 teaspoon pepper
- 12 (6-inch) corn tortillas, divided
- 2 cups shredded Cheddar Monterey Jack cheese blend, divided

Preparation

- Preheat oven in Convection Bake to 375°F (*350°F).
- In skillet, cook ground beef and onion until beef is browned. Drain. Stir in corn, enchilada sauce, tomato sauce, chilies, picanté sauce, oregano, salt and pepper.
- Place 6 tortillas on bottom of 3-quart (9" x 13") baking dish, arranging so that tortillas extend 1-inch up sides of dish. Pour half of meat mixture over tortillas. Top with half of cheese.
- Repeat layers of tortillas, meat mixture.
- Convection Bake for 25 minutes.
- Top with remaining cheese and Convection Bake an additional 10-15 minutes or until hot and bubbly.

Note: Enter this temperature if your oven does not reduce the oven convection temperature automatically by 25°F in the display.

SPICY WILD RICE CASSEROLE

Ingredients

- 1 lb. hot bulk sausage
- 1/2 cup chopped celery
- 1/2 cup chopped onion
- 1/2 cup sliced mushrooms
- 1/2 cup chopped green pepper
- 1 1/2 cups water
- 1 (10 3/4 oz.) can cream of mushroom soup
- 1 (6 oz.) pkg. long grain and wild rice with seasoning packet
- 1 cup shredded Cheddar cheese

Preparation

- Preheat oven in Convection Bake to 375°F (*350°F).
- In skillet, cook sausage, celery, onion, mushrooms and green pepper until meat is browned and vegetables are tender. Drain. Add water, soup, rice and cheese. Spoon mixture into 2-quart (7" x 11") baking dish.
- Cover with foil and convection Bake for 50 to 60 minutes until rice is tender.
- Remove foil and Convection Bake for an additional 5-10 minutes.

VEGETABLE LASAGNA

Ingredients

- 1 large chopped onion
- 1/2 lb. shredded carrots
- 1/2 lb. coarsely chopped fresh mushrooms
- 2 tablespoons vegetable oil
- 2 cups small curd cottage cheese
- 2 eggs
- 1/4 cup grated Parmesan cheese
- 1 teaspoon oregano
- 1 (15 1/2 oz.) jar spaghetti sauce, divided
- 6 cooked lasagna noodles
- 1 (10 oz.) pkg. frozen chopped spinach, thawed and drained
- 1/2 lb. peeled and coarsely chopped tomatoes
- 2 cups shredded mozzarella cheese

Preparation

- Preheat oven in Convection Bake to 375°F (*350°F).
- Sauté onion, carrots and mushrooms in oil over medium-high heat until tender. Drain and set aside.
- In small mixing bowl, combine cottage cheese, eggs, Parmesan cheese and oregano.
- In 2-quart (7" x 11")baking dish, layer half of spaghetti sauce, 3 lasagna noodles, all onion/carrot/mushroom mixture and half of cheese mixture. Cover with remaining noodles, spaghetti sauce, spinach and remaining cheese mixture.
- Top with tomatoes and mozzarella cheese.
- Convection Bake for 35 to 45 minutes or until bubbly. Let stand 10 minutes before serving.

Spread half of cheese mixture over mixed vegetables to form first layer.

Form the second layer with remaining ingredients, starting with the noodles.

*Note: Enter this temperature if your oven does not reduce the oven convection temperature automatically by 25°F in the display.

Cheesy Tuna Tater Pie

Ingredients

CRUST

1 Pillsbury® Refrigerated Pie Crust (from 15 oz. pkg.), softened as directed on package

FILLING

3/4 cup Hungry Jack® Mashed Potato Flakes

1½ cups shredded Cheddar cheese

2 tablespoons chopped pimiento-stuffed green olives

1 (10¾ oz.) can condensed cream of mushroom soup

1 (6 oz.) can water-packed tuna, drained and flaked

1 egg

½ cup canned french fried onions, optional

Preparation

• Preheat oven in Convection Bake to 400°F (*375°F).

• Prepare pie crust as directed on package for one-crust baked shell using 9-inch pie pan.

• Convection Bake for 5 minutes.

• In medium bowl, combine potato flakes, 1 cup of the cheese, olives, soup, tuna and egg; mix well.

• Remove partially baked shell from oven. Spoon filling into shell. Return to oven. Bake an additional 15 minutes.

• Sprinkle top of pie with remaining ½ cup cheese and french fried onions. Convection Bake an additional 10 to 15 minutes or until cheese is melted and onions begin to brown. Let stand 5 minutes before serving.

Reprinted with permission of Pillsbury Company. Adapted by General Electric for convection ovens.

Baked Chicken Salad

Ingredients

2 cups buttery cracker crumbs

¼ cup melted butter

2½ cups finely chopped cooked chicken

1 cup thinly sliced celery

3/4 cup shredded carrots

½ cup chopped onion

½ cup toasted slivered almonds

1 (10-3/4 oz.) can cream of chicken soup

2/3 cup mayonnaise

¼ teaspoon salt

Preparation

• Preheat oven in Convection Bake to 400°F (*375°F).

• Combine buttery cracker crumbs and melted butter. Mix well and set aside.

• Combine chicken, celery, carrots, onion, almonds, soup, mayonnaise and salt. Mix well. Spoon into a 1½ quart baking dish.

• Convection Bake for 30 to 40 minutes or until golden brown and bubbly. Top with cracker crumbs during last 5 minutes of bake time.

Note: Enter this temperature if your oven does not reduce the oven convection temperature automatically by 25°F in the display.

BLACK BEAN
ENCHILADA CASSEROLE

Ingredients

- 1 lb. lean ground beef
- 1 (1.25 oz.) pkg. Old El Paso® Taco Seasoning Mix
- 2/3 cup water
- 1 tablespoon oil
- 1/2 cup chopped onion
- 2 cloves minced garlic
- 1 (15 oz.) can black beans, rinsed and drained
- 1 (10 oz.) can Old El Paso® Enchilada Sauce
- 1 (4.5 oz.) can Old El Paso® chopped Green Chilies
- 1/3 cup sour cream
- 7 or 8 Old El Paso Flour Tortillas for Soft Tacos and Fajitas (from 10.5 oz. pkg.)
- 4 oz. shredded sharp Cheddar cheese
- 2 to 3 oz. crumbled chevre (goat) cheese
- 1 cup Old El Paso® Thick'n Chunky Salsa
- 3 chopped green onions

Preparation

- Preheat oven in Convection Bake to 400°F (*375°F).

- Brown ground beef in large skillet, stirring frequently. Drain. Add taco seasoning mix and water. Mix well. Cook 2 to 4 minutes or until mixture is thickened, stirring occasionally.

- Heat oil in saucepan over medium heat until hot. Add onion and garlic. Cook and stir 3 to 4 minutes or until tender. Add beans, enchilada sauce and green chilies. Mix well. Bring to a boil, stirring occasionally. Remove from heat. Stir in sour cream.

- Spoon ground beef mixture down center of each tortilla. Roll up. Place seam side down in ungreased 2-quart (7" x 11") baking dish.

- Spoon bean and enchilada sauce mixture over filled tortillas. Sprinkle with cheeses.

- Convection Bake for 10 to 20 minutes or until cheeses are melted and casserole is thoroughly heated. Spoon salsa down center of casserole. Sprinkle with green onions.

Reprinted with permission of Pillsbury Company. Adapted by General Electric for convection ovens.

__Note:__ Enter this temperature if your oven does not reduce the oven convection temperature automatically by 25°F in the display.

Spinach and
Cheese-Stuffed Manicotti–page 58

SPINACH QUICHE

Ingredients

- 1 (9-inch) baked deep-dish pie crust
- 2³/₄ cups sliced fresh mushrooms
- 1 tablespoon butter
- 1 (12 oz.) pkg. thawed, frozen spinach soufflé
- ¹/₂ lb. sweet Italian sausage, cooked and crumbled
- ³/₄ cup shredded Swiss cheese
- 2 beaten eggs
- 3 tablespoons whipping cream
- ¹/₂ teaspoon pepper
- ¹/₂ teaspoon hot sauce

Preparation

- Bake crust according to package directions.
- Preheat oven in Convection Bake to 375°F (*350°F).
- In skillet, sauté mushrooms in butter until tender. Drain well.
- Combine mushrooms, spinach soufflé, sausage, cheese, eggs, cream, pepper and hot sauce. Pour into baked crust.
- Convection Bake for 35 to 40 minutes or until knife inserted in center comes out clean. Let stand 10 minutes before serving.

GARLIC CHEESE AND GRITS CASSEROLE
MAKES 6 SERVINGS

Ingredients

- 3 cups hot water
- ³/₄ cup quick cooking grits
- ³/₄ teaspoon salt
- 5 tablespoons sliced butter
- 1¹/₂ cups shredded sharp cheddar cheese
- 2 eggs
- Milk
- ¹/₄ teaspoon garlic powder
- Dash hot sauce
- ¹/₂ cup shredded sharp cheddar cheese
- Paprika

Preparation

- Preheat oven in Convection Bake to 400°F (*375°F).
- Microwave water, grits, and salt in a large bowl at HIGH for 10 to 12 minutes. Stir after 5 minutes. Add butter and 1¹/₂ cups cheese to grits. Stir well until melted.
- Beat eggs. Add enough milk to total ³/₄ cup. Add garlic powder and hot sauce. Quickly stir into grits.
- Pour into well-greased 8-inch square baking dish. Sprinkle ¹/₂ cup cheese over top. Sprinkle with paprika.
- Convection Bake for 25 to 35 minutes or until knife inserted in center comes out clean.

*Note: Enter this temperature if your oven does not reduce the oven convection temperature automatically by 25°F in the display.

EGGS AND CHEESE   **55**

BREAKFAST CHEESE PIZZA

Ingredients

- 1 cup finely chopped fresh mushrooms
- 6 chopped green onions
- 2 tablespoons melted butter
- 6 to 7 slices buttered bread
- 2 cups shredded cheddar cheese
- 2 cups shredded Swiss cheese
- 4 tablespoons all-purpose flour
- 12 slices cooked and crumbled bacon
- 12 eggs
- 2 cups milk
- 1/4 teaspoon salt
- 1/2 teaspoon pepper

Preparation

- Preheat oven in Convection Bake to 375°F (*350°F).
- Sauté mushrooms and onions in butter until tender. Set aside.
- Butter bread slices and place in the bottom of a 3-quart (9" x 13") baking dish, cutting to fit. Sprinkle mushroom mixture over bread.
- Combine cheeses, flour and bacon. Spread over mushroom mixture.
- Beat together eggs, milk, salt and pepper. Pour evenly over cheese mixture.
- Convection bake for 25 to 35 minutes until puffed, lightly browned and knife inserted in center comes out clean.

VEGETABLE FRITTATA

Ingredients

- 1 small thinly sliced onion
- 1/2 small thinly sliced zucchini
- 1/2 cup sliced fresh mushrooms
- 4 asparagus spears, cut into 1/2-inch pieces
- 2 tablespoons melted butter
- 8 beaten eggs
- 1/2 cup milk
- 1/4 teaspoon salt
- 1/8 teaspoon pepper
- Dash hot sauce

Preparation

- Preheat oven in Convection Bake to 375°F (*350°F).
- Place onion, zucchini, mushrooms, asparagus and butter in 9-inch deep pie pan or quiche dish. Microwave at HIGH 3 to 4 minutes or until crisp tender.
- In small mixing bowl, combine eggs, milk, salt, pepper and hot sauce. Blend well. Pour over vegetables.
- Convection Bake for 25 to 40 minutes or until center is set.

*Note: Enter this temperature if your oven does not reduce the oven convection temperature automatically by 25°F in the display.

Pepper Cheese Focaccia

Ingredients

- 1 thinly sliced medium onion
- ½ cup 2-inch thin strips sweet red pepper
- ½ cup 2-inch thin strips green pepper
- 2 tablespoons olive oil
- ½ teaspoon hot sauce
- 2 (8 oz.) pkgs. crescent rolls
- ½ cup grated Parmesan cheese
- 1 lb. shredded Monterey Jack cheese

Preparation

- Preheat oven in Convection Bake to 350°F (*325°F).
- Sauté onion, red pepper and green pepper in olive oil until crisp-tender. Stir in hot sauce. Set aside.
- Grease a 15" x 10" x 1" jellyroll pan. Press crescent roll dough onto jelly roll pan.
- Convection Bake for 5 minutes. Sprinkle with Parmesan cheese. Top with onion mixture and Monterey Jack cheese. Bake for additional 15 minutes or until cheese begins to brown.

Macaroni and Cheese

Ingredients

- 1 (7 oz.) pkg. elbow macaroni
- 2 cups shredded sharp cheddar cheese
- 1 (3 oz.) pkg. softened cream cheese
- 2 tablespoons butter
- 2 cups milk
- 1 teaspoon Worcestershire sauce
- 2 tablespoons all-purpose flour
- 1 teaspoon salt
- ⅛ teaspoon pepper

Preparation

- Preheat oven in Convection Bake to 375°F (*350°F).
- Cook macaroni according to package directions. Drain. Combine macaroni, cheddar cheese, cream cheese and butter in lightly greased 2-quart casserole.
- Combine milk, Worcestershire sauce, flour, salt and pepper. Stir to blend. Pour over macaroni mixture.
- Convection Bake for 35 to 40 minutes until bubbly.

HAM AND EGG CASSEROLE

Ingredients

- 3 cups white bread cubes, crusts removed
- 2 cups shredded sharp cheddar cheese
- 1/4 cup finely chopped green onion
- 1 (41/2 oz.) can sliced mushrooms, drained
- 1 cup cubed (1/2" cubes) ham
- 4 eggs
- 1/2 cup milk
- 1 teaspoon dry mustard
- 1/8 teaspoon pepper
- Dash hot sauce

Preparation

- Preheat oven in Convection Bake to 375°F (*350°F).
- Remove crusts and cube enough bread to make 3 cups.
- In 2-quart (7" x 11") baking dish, place cubed bread. Sprinkle cheese, green onion and mushrooms over bread. Top with ham cubes.
- Beat together eggs, milk, dry mustard, pepper and hot sauce. Pour egg mixture over bread, cheese and ham.
- Convection Bake for 30 to 40 minutes or until knife inserted in center comes out clean.

SPINACH AND CHEESE-STUFFED MANICOTTI

Stuff cooked manicotti with spinach and cheese filling.

Ingredients

- 10 manicotti noodles
- 1 cup shredded mozzarella cheese
- 2 cups ricotta cheese
- 1/2 cup Romano cheese
- 1 (73/4 oz.) can spinach, drained
- 1/2 teaspoon garlic powder
- 1/2 teaspoon salt
- 1/4 teaspoon pepper

TOPPING

- 1 (15 oz.) can tomato sauce
- 1/8 teaspoon sweet basil
- 1/8 teaspoon oregano
- 1 cup shredded mozzarella cheese

Preparation

- Preheat oven in Convection Bake to 375°F (*350°F).
- Cook manicotti noodles according to package directions.
- Combine mozzarella, ricotta, Romano, spinach, garlic powder, salt and pepper. Stuff cooked manicotti with cheese filling. Arrange in 3-quart (9" x 13") baking dish. Set aside.
- Combine tomato sauce, basil and oregano. Pour over manicotti. Sprinkle with mozzarella cheese.
- Convection Bake for 30 to 35 minutes or until bubbly.

Note: Enter this temperature if your oven does not reduce the oven convection temperature automatically by 25°F in the display.

CORN AND CHEESE SOUFFLÉ

Ingredients

- ¼ **cup melted butter**
- ¼ **cup all-purpose flour**
- ¼ **teaspoon salt**
- ⅛ **teaspoon white pepper**
- 1½ **cups milk**
- 2¼ **cups shredded cheddar cheese**
- 1 **(8 oz.) can whole kernel corn, drained**
- 6 **eggs, separated**

Preparation

- Preheat oven in Convection Bake to 350°F (*325°F).
- Combine melted butter, flour, salt and pepper in a large bowl. Gradually stir in milk. Microwave at MEDIUM HIGH for 4 to 6 minutes, until slightly thickened, stirring every 2 minutes. Add cheese and corn. Microwave at MEDIUM HIGH for 2 minutes. Stir to blend.
- Beat egg yolks. To prevent eggs from cooking in hard lumps when added into sauce, stir a small amount of the cheese sauce into the egg yolks. Add egg yolk mixture to remainder of sauce, blending well. Cool slightly.
- Beat egg whites until soft peaks form. With a rubber spatula, fold egg whites into cheese sauce just until blended. Pour into greased 2-quart soufflé dish.
- Convection Bake for 35 to 45 minutes or until top is puffed and golden and center is set. Serve immediately.

Beat egg whites until soft peaks form.

Gently fold egg whites into cheese sauce .

> ### Cooking Tip
>
> Like all egg mixtures, custards are delicate and don't like high heat. They thicken at a low temperature. You'll have beautiful, trouble free custards as long as you insulate the eggs from the heat: first, when you add the eggs to the hot liquid and second, when you cook the mixture. To prepare the eggs to withstand hot liquid, beat them slightly in a small bowl. Then beat in a little of the hot liquid. Now they are warmed and you can safely beat them into the rest of the hot liquid.

ASPARAGUS AND CHEESE BRUNCH

Ingredients

- 8 **slices bread**
- 1 **(16 oz.) can drained asparagus, cut into 2-inch pieces**
- 2 **cups shredded cheddar cheese**
- 4 **beaten eggs**
- 2 **cups milk**
- 2 **tablespoons minced onion**
- 1½ **teaspoons salt**
- ¼ **teaspoon dry mustard**
- ¼ **teaspoon paprika**
- ⅛ **teaspoon pepper**

Preparation

- Preheat oven in Convection Bake to 375°F (*350°F).
- Remove crusts from bread and cut into cubes.
- In 2-quart (7" x 11") baking dish, arrange half the bread. Cover with asparagus and sprinkle with cheddar cheese. Cover with remaining bread.
- Combine eggs, milk, onion, salt, mustard, paprika and pepper. Pour mixture over casserole. Let stand 20 minutes.
- Convection Bake for 40 to 50 minutes or until puffed and lightly browned. Let stand 5 minutes before serving.

*__*Note:__ Enter this temperature if your oven does not reduce the oven convection temperature automatically by 25°F in the display.*

VEGETABLES

Green Bean
Casserole–page 62

Acorn Squash

Ingredients

- 3 medium acorn squash
- 2½ cups water
- 1-2 tablespoons brown sugar
- 1-2 tablespoons butter for each half of acorn squash

Preparation

- Preheat oven in Convection Bake to 375°F (*350°F).
- Wash acorn squash. Cut in half and remove seeds. Place cut side down in a 3 quart (9" x 13") baking dish. Add water approximately ½-inch deep in dish.
- Convection Bake for 25-30 minutes. Turn over and add brown sugar, butter, and choice of filling mixture. Return to oven and continue baking for 10 to 15 minutes.

Filling Selections
- 2 tablespoons crushed pineapple
- 1 tablespoon chopped apple
- ¼ cup apple pie filling
- 2 tablespoons chopped mandarin oranges

Scalloped Potatoes

MAKES 8 SERVINGS

Ingredients

- ¼ cup melted butter
- ¼ cup all-purpose flour
- 2 cups milk
- 1 tablespoon dried onion flakes
- 1 teaspoon salt
- ¼ teaspoon pepper
- 6 peeled and thinly sliced medium potatoes

Preparation

- Preheat oven in Convection Bake to 375°F (*350°F).
- In 4-cup glass measure, combine melted butter and flour. Gradually add milk, stirring until smooth. Add onion flakes, salt and pepper. Microwave at MEDIUM HIGH (7) for 7 to 9 minutes, stirring every 3 minutes until sauce is smooth and slightly thickened.
- In 2-quart (7" x 11") baking dish, alternate potatoes and sauce.
- Convection Bake for 30 to 40 minutes or until tender. Let stand 5 minutes before serving.

Classic Baked Beans

MAKES 6 TO 8 SERVINGS

Ingredients

- 2 (16 oz.) cans baked beans
- ½ cup finely chopped onion
- ¼ cup catsup
- 2 tablespoons brown sugar
- 3 slices bacon, cooked crisp and crumbled
- 2 teaspoons prepared mustard
- 1 teaspoon Worcestershire Sauce

Preparation

- Preheat oven in Convection Bake to 375°F (*350°F).
- In 8-inch square baking dish, combine beans, onion, catsup, sugar, bacon, mustard and Worcestershire Sauce. Mix well.
- Convection Bake for 20 to 30 minutes or until bubbly.

GREEN BEAN CASSEROLE

Ingredients

- **2 (15 oz.) cans French-style green beans**
- **1 (10 3/4 oz.) can cream of mushroom soup**
- **1/2 cup milk**
- **1 (2 oz.) jar sliced pimiento, drained**
- **1/2 teaspoon salt**
- **1/2 teaspoon pepper**
- **1 (3 oz.) can coarsely crushed French-fried onions**

Preparation

- Preheat oven in Convection Bake to 375°F (*350°F).
- Combine beans, soup, milk, pimiento, salt and pepper. Spoon mixture into 2-quart (7" x 11") baking dish.
- Convection Bake for 25 to 35 minutes.
- Sprinkle with onions. Continue baking for 5 minutes or until onions are brown.

Cooking Tip

It's difficult to improve on an old favorite, but this variation is a flavorful change. Use 1 can cream of celery soup instead of mushroom soup. Replace the pimiento with an 8 oz. can of sliced water chestnuts, drained.

2 (16 oz.) packages of frozen French-style green beans may be substituted for the canned green beans.

CANDIED SWEET POTATOES

Ingredients

- **2 (15 oz.) cans sweet potatoes, drained and cut up**
- **1/2 cup packed brown sugar**
- **Dash nutmeg**
- **3 tablespoons butter, cut into small pieces**
- **1/4 cup toasted chopped pecans**

Preparation

- Preheat oven in Convection Bake to 375°F (*350°F).
- In medium microwave safe bowl, melt butter. Add brown sugar, nutmeg and pecans. Mix well. Add potatoes and mix until coated. Pour into 1 1/2 quart baking dish.
- Convection Bake for 15 to 25 minutes until heated through.

Cooking Tip

To make this recipe with fresh sweet potatoes, cook 2 pounds sweet potatoes in enough boiling water to cover for 30 minutes or until tender; drain. Cool slightly, then peel and cut into 1/2-inch thick slices. Never store fresh uncooked sweet potatoes in the refrigerator. They lose flavor and turn black in cool temperatures.

Cooking Tip

Toasting nuts really brings out the flavor. Spread in a single layer on a baking sheet and toast at 350°F for 3 to 5 minutes, or stir in a dry, heavy skillet over low heat for 2 or 3 minutes. Watch closely. Be ready to remove from oven or heat as soon as they start to color.

*Note: Enter this temperature if your oven does not reduce the oven convection temperature automatically by 25°F in the display.

CORN PUDDING

Ingredients

2 tablespoons melted butter

2 tablespoons all-purpose flour

2 tablespoons sugar

1/2 teaspoon salt

1 cup milk

3 beaten eggs

1 (16 oz.) can whole kernel corn, drained

Preparation

• Preheat oven in Convection Bake to 350°F (*325°F).

• In 1 1/2-quart casserole, combine butter, flour, sugar, salt, milk, eggs and corn.

• Convection Bake for 25 to 35 minutes or until center is barely set.

PARMESAN CHEESE POTATO SLICES

Ingredients

3 large baking potatoes, sliced 1/4-inch thick

1/2 cup grated Parmesan cheese

1/8 teaspoon paprika

3 tablespoons melted butter

1/2 teaspoon salt

Preparation

• Preheat oven in Convection Bake to 375°F (*350°F).

• Place sliced potatoes on 3 baking sheets. Combine Parmesan cheese and paprika. Brush potato slices with butter and sprinkle with Parmesan cheese mixture.

• Convection Bake for 30 to 35 minutes or until browned.

SPINACH WITH ARTICHOKES CASSEROLE

Ingredients

1 (8 oz.) pkg. softened cream cheese

4 tablespoons softened butter

2 tablespoons mayonnaise

6 tablespoons milk

1 (14 oz.) can artichoke hearts, drained and chopped

2 (10 oz.) pkgs. frozen chopped spinach, thawed and drained

1/3 cup grated Parmesan cheese

Dash pepper

Preparation

• Preheat oven in Convection Bake to 375°F (*350°F).

• Combine cream cheese, butter and mayonnaise. Beat with an electric mixer for 2 minutes until light and fluffy. Gradually beat in milk.

• In 2-quart (7" x 11") baking dish, place chopped artichokes in bottom of pan. Spoon spinach evenly over artichokes. Spread cream cheese mixture over spinach. Sprinkle with Parmesan cheese and pepper.

• Convection Bake for 25 to 35 minutes or until top is lightly browned.

*Note: Enter this temperature if your oven does not reduce the oven convection temperature automatically by 25°F in the display.

Ingredients

- **1 large eggplant, peeled and sliced**
- **1 teaspoon olive oil**
- **1/2 cup finely chopped onion**
- **1/2 cup finely chopped green pepper**
- **1/2 cup finely chopped celery**
- **2 (8 oz.) cans tomato sauce**
- **1 1/2 teaspoons oregano**
- **1 1/2 teaspoons basil**
- **1/2 teaspoon garlic salt**
- **1 1/2 cups shredded cheddar cheese**
- **1/4 cup grated Parmesan Cheese**

Preparation

- Preheat oven in Convection Bake to 375°F (*350°F).
- Microwave eggplant with small amount of water, covered with plastic wrap, until tender. Drain.
- In a large skillet coated with 1 teaspoon olive oil, cook onions green pepper and celery until crisp tender. Add tomato sauce, oregano, basil and garlic salt. Blend well.
- Spread 3 tablespoons sauce on bottom of 2-quart baking dish. Layer half of eggplant, half of remaining sauce and half the cheddar cheese. Repeat layers. Top with Parmesan cheese.
- Convection Bake for 20 to 30 minutes or until bubbly and cheese is melted.

STUFFED YELLOW SQUASH   MAKES 6 SERVINGS

Scoop out pulp and seeds leaving 1/4-inch thick shell.

Ingredients

- **3 large yellow squash**
- **1/4 lb. hot bulk sausage**
- **1/2 cup chopped green pepper**
- **1/4 cup chopped onion**
- **1 medium chopped tomato**
- **1/2 cup grated Parmesan cheese**
- **1 cup shredded mozzarella cheese**

Preparation

- Preheat oven in Convection Bake to 350°F (*325°F).
- Cut squash in half, lengthwise. Scoop out pulp and seeds; discard, leaving 1/4-inch thick shell. Set aside.
- Cook sausage, green pepper and onion until meat is browned. Drain. Add tomato and Parmesan cheese. Stir until well blended.
- Place squash in 3-quart (9" x 13") baking dish. Divide sausage mixture evenly among squash shells and top with mozzarella cheese.
- Convection Bake for 20 minutes or until cheese is melted and lightly browned.

Variations

Substitute hamburger for sausage.

Vegetarian: Combine onions, peppers, tomatoes, cheese, salt, pepper and seasonings such as crushed red pepper seeds.

Note: Enter this temperature if your oven does not reduce the oven convection temperature automatically by 25°F in the display.

CHEESY BROCCOLI

Ingredients

- **1 cup instant rice**
- **1 (10¾ oz.) can condensed cream of chicken soup**
- **½ cup milk**
- **1 (8 oz.) jar processed cheese spread**
- **¼ teaspoon pepper**
- **1 (10 oz.) pkg. frozen chopped broccoli, cooked and drained**
- **½ cup chopped celery**
- **¼ cup chopped onion**

Preparation

- Preheat oven in Convection Bake to 375°F (*350°F).
- In 2-quart casserole, combine rice, soup, milk, cheese and pepper. Microwave on HIGH for 2 to 4 minutes until cheese melts and can be blended easily. Add broccoli, celery and onion to the cheese mixture. Stir thoroughly.
- Convection Bake for 20 to 30 minutes or until bubbly.

TWICE-BAKED POTATOES

Ingredients

- **2 large baking potatoes**
- **2 tablespoons butter**
- **¼ cup milk**
- **½ teaspoon salt**
- **¼ teaspoon garlic powder**
- **⅛ teaspoon pepper**
- **½ cup shredded cheddar cheese**

Preparation

- Preheat oven in Convection Bake to 425°F (*400°F).
- Wash potatoes thoroughly. Pat dry. Prick skins with a fork.
- Convection Bake directly on the oven rack for 45 to 50 minutes or until potatoes are tender.
- Cut cooked potatoes in half. Scoop out potatoes leaving ¼-inch thick shell. Set aside.
- Combine scooped out potato, butter, milk, salt, garlic powder and pepper. Whip with electric mixer at high speed for 1 minute or until smooth.
- Place potato shells in an 8-inch square baking dish and fill with whipped potato mixture. Sprinkle Cheddar cheese on top.
- Convection Bake for 15 to 20 minutes or until heated through.

Note: *Enter this temperature if your oven does not reduce the oven convection temperature automatically by 25°F in the display.*

Ingredients

- 6 coarsely chopped yellow squash
- 1/2 cup water
- 2 dozen crushed round buttery crackers
- 1 (3 oz.) pkg. softened cream cheese
- 1 (10 3/4 oz.) can cream of chicken soup
- 1 egg
- 1/4 cup melted butter
- 3 small grated carrots
- 1/2 cup finely chopped onion

Preparation

- Preheat oven in Convection Bake to 375°F (*350°F).
- Combine squash and water. Cover with plastic and microwave 5 minutes. Drain well and set aside.
- Place half of crackers in bottom of greased 2-quart (7" x 11") baking dish.
- Combine cream cheese, soup, egg and butter. Beat with electric mixer at high speed for 1 minute. Stir in squash, carrots and onion. Spoon into cracker-lined baking dish, and sprinkle with remaining cracker crumbs.
- Convection Bake for 30 to 40 minutes or until bubbly and heated through.

IOWA CORN STUFFED TOMATOES

Ingredients

- 1 1/2 cups Green Giant® Niblets® Frozen Corn
- 4 medium tomatoes
  Pepper
- 4 oz. (1 cup) shredded cheddar cheese
- 2 tablespoons Progresso® Plain Bread Crumbs
- 1/4 cup chopped green pepper
- 1 thinly sliced green onion
- 3 tablespoons melted margarine or butter

Preparation

- Preheat oven in Convection Bake to 375°F (*350°F).
- Cook corn as directed on package.
- Cut tomatoes in half crosswise. With spoon, carefully remove and discard seeds. Sprinkle cut surface of tomato halves with pepper.
- Combine cooked corn and all remaining ingredients. Fill tomato halves with corn mixture. Place stuffed tomatoes in ungreased 3-quart (9" x 13") baking dish.
- Convection Bake for 10 to 20 minutes or until thoroughly heated.

Reprinted with permission of Pillsbury Company. Adapted by General Electric for convection ovens.

Note: Enter this temperature if your oven does not reduce the oven convection temperature automatically by 25°F in the display.

BREADS

Braided Egg Bread—page 71

FRUITY ORANGE
REFRIGERATOR MUFFINS

Ingredients

1½ **cups all-purpose flour**

1 **cup whole wheat flour**

2 **cups wheat bran cereal**

1½ **cups sugar**

1¼ **teaspoons baking soda**

1 **teaspoon baking powder**

½ **teaspoon salt**

¼ **teaspoon allspice**

1 **tablespoon grated orange peel**

2½ **cups buttermilk**

½ **cup oil**

2 **slightly beaten eggs**

1 **(6 oz.) pkg. dried fruit pieces**

Preparation

- In large bowl, combine all-purpose flour, whole wheat flour, cereal, sugar, baking soda, baking powder, salt, allspice and orange peel. Mix well. Add buttermilk, oil and eggs. Blend well. Stir in fruit. Cover tightly. Refrigerate at least 3 hours before using.

- Preheat oven in Convection Bake to 400°F (*375°F).

- Grease desired number of muffin cups or line with paper baking cups. Stir batter. Fill greased muffin cups ¾ full.

- Convection Bake for 15 to 25 minutes or until toothpick inserted in center comes out clean. Immediately remove from pan. Serve warm.

Cooking Tip

As a substitute for each cup of buttermilk, you can use 1 tablespoon vinegar or lemon juice plus whole milk to equal 1 cup (let stand 10 minutes) or until thickened.

About Muffin Pans

- To date, muffin pans have not been manufactured with an absolute standard size. The cup size of older muffin pans tends to be larger than more recently manufactured pans. Both old and new are likely to yield smaller muffins than the mega-sized treats, found in many bakeries. Smaller muffin pans and those with a dark metal finish will require less baking time. Fill the muffin cups ⅔ to ¾ full with batter. To check for doneness, insert a toothpick into the center of the muffin. If the toothpick comes out clean, the muffin is done.

Cooking Tip

Rich with texture from whole-bran cereal and dried fruit, this muffin batter is great to have on hand for baking a warm treat in the morning. Mix the batter in advance and bake just the amount needed. Batter will keep in refrigerator up to 2 weeks.

Reprinted with permission of Pillsbury Company. Adapted by General Electric for convection ovens.

***Note:** Enter this temperature if your oven does not reduce the oven convection temperature automatically by 25°F in the display.*

HERB PULL-APART BREAD

MAKES 6 SERVINGS

Place rounds so that they slightly overlap.

Ingredients

- **1 (7 oz.) can refrigerated soft breadsticks**
- **1 tablespoon melted margarine or butter**
- **1/4 teaspoon dried basil**
- **1/4 teaspoon dried thyme**

Preparation

- Preheat oven in Convection Bake to 375°F (*350°F).
- Separate dough into 6 rounds, do not unroll.
- Place rounds on cookie sheet, slightly overlapping as shown in diagram.
- In small bowl, combine margarine, basil and thyme. Brush margarine mixture over top of bread rounds.
- Convection Bake at 350° for 15 to 20 minutes or until golden brown. Serve warm.

Variations

Basil and thyme is just one flavor combination for the soft breadstick dough. Other possibilities include: Garlic powder and black pepper. Hot chili powder. Oregano, salt and pepper. Sage and marjoram. Dill weed. Minced fresh garlic and fresh parsley. Cinnamon, nutmeg and sugar.

Reprinted with permission of Pillsbury Company. Adapted by General Electric for convection ovens.

PEPPER BISCUIT PULL-APART

MAKES 10 SERVINGS

Ingredients

- **1/4 teaspoon garlic powder**
- **1/4 teaspoon salt, if desired**
- **1/4 teaspoon crushed dried basil**
- **1/4 teaspoon crushed dried oregano**
- **1 (12 oz.) can refrigerated flaky biscuits**
- **4 1/2 teaspoons olive oil**
- **1/4 cup chopped green pepper**
- **1/4 cup chopped red pepper**
- **1/4 cup shredded mozzarella cheese**
- **2 tablespoons grated Romano or Parmesan cheese**

Preparation

- Preheat oven in Convection Bake to 400°F (*375°F).
- In small bowl, combine garlic powder, salt, basil and oregano. Blend well and side aside.
- Separate dough into 10 biscuits. Place 1 biscuit in center of ungreased cookie sheet. Arrange remaining biscuits in a circle, edges slightly overlapping around center biscuit. Gently press out to 10-inch circle.
- Brush with olive oil. Top with bell peppers and cheeses. Sprinkle garlic powder mixture over top.
- Convection Bake for 12 to 15 minutes or until golden brown. To serve, pull part warm biscuits.

Cooking Tip

Serve as a snack or with soup or salad.

Reprinted with permission of Pillsbury Company. Adapted by General Electric for convection ovens.

***Note:** Enter this temperature if your oven does not reduce the oven convection temperature automatically by 25°F in the display.*

Savory Cheese and Scallion Scones

Ingredients

SCONES
- 2³/4 cups all-purpose flour
- 5 teaspoons baking powder
- ¹/2 teaspoon salt, optional
- 4 oz. crumbled feta cheese
- 4 oz. cream cheese, cut into 1-inch cubes
- 4 chopped scallions or green onions
- 1 cup half and half or milk
- 1 egg

GLAZE
- 1 egg
- 2 tablespoons milk

Preparation
- Preheat oven in Convection Bake to 400°F (*375°F).
- Grease large cookie sheet.
- In large bowl, combine flour, baking powder and salt. Mix well. With pastry blender or fork, cut in feta cheese and cream cheese until mixture is crumbly. Add scallions and toss gently until combined.
- In small bowl, combine half and half and egg. Blend well. Add half and half mixture to flour mixture. Stir lightly, just until soft dough forms. Turn dough onto well floured surface. Knead lightly 5 or 6 times. Pat or press dough into 1 inch thick round.
- With floured knife, cut into 8 wedges. Place wedges 2 inches apart on greased cookie sheet.
- Before baking, the scones may be glazed.
- Combine glaze ingredients. Blend well. Brush over tops of wedges.
- Convection bake at 375° for 20 to 25 minutes or until golden brown. Remove scones from cookie sheet. Cool 5 minutes. Serve warm or cool. Store in refrigerator.

Reprinted with permission of Pillsbury Company. Adapted by General Electric for convection ovens.

Hearty Nut Muffins

Ingredients
- 3 cups all-purpose flour
- 1¹/2 cups coarsely chopped pecans
- 1 cup uncooked oats
- 1 cup corn flakes
- 1 tablespoon baking powder
- 2 teaspoons baking soda
- ¹/2 teaspoon salt
- 2 cups mashed ripe banana
- 1 cup milk
- 1 cup honey
- 4 tablespoons melted butter
- 1 egg

Preparation
- Preheat oven in Convection Bake to 400°F (*375°F).
- In large mixing bowl, combine flour, pecans, oats, corn flakes, baking powder, baking soda and salt.
- In medium mixing bowl, beat together bananas, milk, honey, butter and egg. Add banana mixture to dry ingredients. Stir until moistened.
- Spoon batter equally into 24 paper-lined muffin cups.
- Convection Bake for 13 to 16 minutes or until golden brown.

Note: Enter this temperature if your oven does not reduce the oven convection temperature automatically by 25°F in the display.

CRANBERRY AND ORANGE SCONES

Ingredients

SCONES

1³/₄ cups all-purpose flour

¹/₄ cup sugar

2 teaspoons baking powder

¹/₄ teaspoon baking soda

¹/₄ teaspoon salt

¹/₄ cup butter

¹/₂ cup sweetened dried cranberries

¹/₂ cup vanilla milk chips

1 teaspoon grated orange peel

¹/₂ cup low-fat yogurt

¹/₃ cup buttermilk

TOPPING

1 to 2 tablespoons buttermilk or milk

1 tablespoon sugar

¹/₂ teaspoon grated orange peel

Preparation

- Preheat oven in Convection Bake to 375°F (*350°F).
- Grease a large cookie sheet.
- In large bowl, combine flour, sugar, baking powder, baking soda and salt. Mix well. With pastry blender or fork, cut in butter until mixture resembles coarse crumbs. Stir in cranberries, vanilla chips and orange peel. Add yogurt and buttermilk. Stir just until moistened.
- Shape dough into ball. Place on greased cookie sheet. Roll or pat dough into 8-inch round. Cut into 8 wedges. Do not separate.
- Brush with 1 to 2 tablespoons buttermilk or milk. In small bowl, combine 1 tablespoon sugar and ¹/₂ teaspoon grated orange peel. Sprinkle over dough.
- Convection Bake for 20 to 30 minutes or until edges begin to turn golden brown. Cool 5 minutes. Cut into wedges. Serve warm or cool.

Reprinted with permission of Pillsbury Company. Adapted by General Electric for convection ovens.

BRAIDED EGG BREAD

Ingredients

2¹/₂ cups all-purpose flour, divided

2 tablespoons sugar

1 (1/4 oz.) pkg. dry yeast

¹/₄ teaspoon salt

²/₃ cup warm water

2 tablespoons butter

1 beaten egg

Preparation

- Preheat oven in Convection Bake to 400°F (*375°F).
- In large mixing bowl, combine 1¹/₂ cups flour, sugar, yeast, salt, water, butter and egg. Beat with electric mixer on medium speed for 2 minutes. Stir in remaining flour to form soft dough.
- Cover. Let rise about 1 hour or until double in size.
- Roll dough out on lightly floured surface into 12" x 6" rectangle. Cut into 3 long pieces 12" x 2" each. Roll each piece into a strand. On lightly greased baking sheet, braid the three strands together to make a loaf.
- Cover. Let rise about 1 hour or until double in size.
- Convection Bake for 13 to 16 minutes until browned and hollow sounding when tapped with fingers.

Note: *Enter this temperature if your oven does not reduce the oven convection temperature automatically by 25°F in the display.*

Ingredients

4 cans buttermilk biscuits

1½ cups sugar

1 tablespoon cinnamon

1½ sticks butter

½ cup chopped pecans or raisins

Preparation

• Preheat oven in Convection Bake to 350°F (*325°F).

• Cut biscuits into fourths with kitchen shears. Mix sugar and cinnamon together. Roll each biscuit piece in sugar/cinnamon mixture until coated.

• In saucepan, melt butter and add sugar/cinnamon mixture left over from coating the biscuits.

• Place half of biscuits in greased Bundt or tube pan. Add pecans and/or raisins. Pour half of melted butter mixture into pan. Add remaining biscuit pieces and pour other half of butter mixture on top.

• Convection Bake for 35 to 40 minutes or until well browned.

Variations

• Add fresh apples or dried fruit.

• Add rum or rum extract or other flavor extracts.

• Butter and herbs and/or spices; omit sugar and cinnamon, may need salt– may use refrigerated breadsticks.

• Add seeds and nuts.

• Add vegetables.

ZUCCHINI BREAD   MAKES ONE 9-INCH LOAF

Ingredients

1¾ cups all-purpose flour

1 teaspoon cinnamon

1 teaspoon baking soda

½ teaspoon salt

1 cup sugar

1 cup grated zucchini

2 eggs

½ cup vegetable oil

½ cup plain yogurt

1½ teaspoons vanilla

1 cup chopped pecans

Preparation

• Preheat oven in Convection Bake to 375°F (*350°F).

• In small mixing bowl, sift together flour, cinnamon, baking soda and salt.

• In medium mixing bowl, combine sugar, zucchini, eggs, oil, yogurt and vanilla. Add flour mixture. Stir well. Fold in nuts. Pour batter into well greased and floured 9" x 5" x 3" loaf pan.

• Convection Bake for 40 to 50 minutes or until toothpick inserted in center comes out clean. Remove from pan and let cool on wire rack.

*Note: Enter this temperature if your oven does not reduce the oven convection temperature automatically by 25°F in the display.

SOUR CREAM BREAD

Ingredients

BREAD

2 cups all-purpose flour

1 cup sugar

1½ teaspoons baking powder

1 teaspoon baking soda

½ cup butter

1 (8 oz.) container sour cream

3 beaten eggs

2½ teaspoons vanilla

¼ teaspoon almond extract

¾ cup chopped pecans

CRUMB TOPPING

⅔ cup all-purpose flour

⅓ cup sugar

⅓ cup butter

Preparation

BREAD

- Preheat oven in Convection Bake to 350°F (*325°F).
- Grease a 9" x 5" x 3" loaf pan. Set aside.
- In large mixing bowl, combine flour, sugar, baking powder and baking soda. Using a pastry blender, cut in butter until mixture resembles coarse crumbs. Blend in sour cream, eggs, vanilla and almond extract. Fold in pecans.
- Pour batter into prepared pan.
- Sprinkle crumb topping over batter.
- Convection Bake for 55 to 65 minutes or until toothpick inserted in center comes out clean.

CRUMB TOPPING

- In small bowl, combine flour and sugar.
- Using a pastry blender, cut in butter until mixture resembles coarse crumbs.

CORN MUFFINS WITH CHILE BUTTER

MAKES 8 SERVINGS

Ingredients

MUFFINS

1 (8½ oz.) pkg. corn muffin mix

⅓ cup milk

1 egg

½ cup shredded cheddar cheese

3 tablespoons finely chopped red pepper

CHILE BUTTER

½ cup softened butter

2 tablespoons chopped fresh cilantro

1 seeded and chopped fresh jalapeño chile

Preparation

MUFFINS

- Preheat oven in Convection Bake to 400°F (*375°F).
- Prepare corn muffin mix as directed on package using milk and egg. Stir in cheese and bell pepper. Divide batter evenly into paper-lined muffin cups.
- Bake for 18 to 22 minutes or until tops are light golden brown and toothpick inserted in center comes out clean. Immediately remove from pan.

CHILE BUTTER

- Using a food processor or mixer, combine all chile butter ingredients. Blend until well mixed. Serve chile butter with warm muffins.

Reprinted with permission of Pillsbury Company. Adapted by General Electric for convection ovens.

Note: *Enter this temperature if your oven does not reduce the oven convection temperature automatically by 25°F in the display.*

Oatmeal-Orange Coffee Cake

MAKES ONE 9-INCH COFFEE CAKE

Ingredients

COFFEE CAKE

- 1½ cups all-purpose flour
- 1 cup regular uncooked rolled oats
- ⅓ cup firmly packed brown sugar
- 1 tablespoon baking powder
- ½ teaspoon baking soda
- 2 ripe mashed bananas
- ½ cup orange juice
- ⅓ cup melted butter
- 1 beaten egg
- ¼ teaspoon grated orange rind
- ½ teaspoon vanilla

ORANGE GLAZE

- ½ cup powdered sugar
- 1 tablespoon orange juice
- ¼ teaspoon grated orange rind

Preparation

COFFEE CAKE

- Preheat oven in Convection Bake to 375°F (*350°F).
- In large mixing bowl, combine flour, oats, brown sugar, baking powder and baking soda.
- Combine bananas, orange juice, butter, egg, orange rind and vanilla. Add to flour mixture stirring just until moistened.
- Pour batter into lightly greased 9-inch round cake pan.
- Convection Bake for 25 to 30 minutes or until golden brown. Cool 10 minutes on wire rack. Remove from pan.

ORANGE GLAZE

- In small mixing bowl, combine powdered sugar, orange juice and orange rind.
- Drizzle evenly over cake while still warm.

Banana Bread

MAKES ONE 9-INCH LOAF

Ingredients

- ¾ cup sugar
- ½ cup butter
- ¾ cup mashed bananas (about 2 medium)
- 2 teaspoons lemon juice
- ⅓ cup milk
- 2 beaten eggs
- 1½ cups all-purpose flour
- 1 teaspoon baking soda
- ½ teaspoon baking powder
- ½ cup chopped walnuts

Preparation

- Preheat oven in Convection Bake to 350°F (*325°F).
- Grease a 9" x 5" x 3" loaf pan. Set aside.
- In large mixing bowl, cream sugar and butter with an electric mixer. Mix in mashed bananas and lemon juice. Add milk and eggs. Sift in flour, baking soda and baking powder. Blend well. Stir in nuts. Pour into prepared pan.
- Convection Bake for 50 to 60 minutes.

Note: Enter this temperature if your oven does not reduce the oven convection temperature automatically by 25°F in the display.

Toasted Coconut Pretzels

MAKES 20-25 PRETZELS

Ingredients

PRETZELS

3 cups all-purpose flour

1/2 cup sliced butter

1 (1/4 oz.) pkg. dry yeast

1/4 cup granulated sugar, divided

1/4 cup warm water

1 cup whipping cream

3 beaten egg yolks

1/2 teaspoon salt

TOPPING

1 egg white

1 cup coconut

1/2 cup firmly packed brown sugar

Preparation

PRETZELS

- Place flour in large mixing bowl. Cut in butter, with a pastry blender, until mixture resembles coarse crumbs. Cover and refrigerate.

- In medium mixing bowl, sprinkle yeast and 1 tablespoon of granulated sugar over warm water. Stir to dissolve. Let stand 5 minutes until foamy. Add cream, egg yolks, salt and remaining sugar. Stir well.

- Pour over flour mixture and stir until flour is just moistened. Cover and refrigerate dough at least 12 hours.

- Preheat oven in Convection Bake to 350°F (*325°F).

- Punch dough down. Roll out on lightly floured surface into 16-inch square. Fold dough over into thirds. Starting on the short side, roll dough out into approximately 10" x 20" rectangle.

- With pizza cutter, cut 10-inch strips approximately 3/4-inch wide. Form each strip into a pretzel shape. Brush each pretzel with egg white. Sprinkle with coconut mixture.

- Convection Bake for 15 to 17 minutes.

TOPPING

- In small mixing bowl, combine coconut and brown sugar. Sprinkle coconut mixture on top of each pretzel.

Note: Enter this temperature if your oven does not reduce the oven convection temperature automatically by 25°F in the display.

Basic White Bread

Ingredients

- 5³/₄ **to 6 cups all-purpose flour, divided**
- 2 **(¹/₄ oz.) pkgs. dry yeast**
- 2¹/₄ **cups milk**
- 3 **tablespoons sugar**
- 3 **tablespoons vegetable shortening**
- 2 **teaspoons salt**

Preparation

- In large mixing bowl, combine 2¹/₂ cups flour and yeast.
- In saucepan, heat and stir milk, sugar, shortening and salt until warm (120° - 130°) and shortening is nearly melted. Add to flour mixture.
- Beat with electric mixer on low speed for 30 seconds, scraping bowl constantly. Beat on high speed for 3 minutes. With a spoon, stir in as much of remaining flour as possible.
- Turn dough onto lightly floured surface. Knead in enough of remaining flour to make a moderately stiff dough that is smooth and elastic (6 to 8 minutes). Shape into a ball. Place in a lightly greased bowl. Turn once to grease surface. Cover. Let rise until double in size.
- Punch dough down. Turn out onto lightly floured surface. Divide dough in half. Cover. Let rest 10 minutes. Shape each half into a loaf. Place shaped dough in two lightly greased 8" x 4" x 2" loaf pans. Cover. Let rise until nearly double in size (30 to 40 minutes).
- Preheat oven in Convection Bake to 350°F (*325°F).
- Convection Bake for 30 to 35 minutes or until done. Remove from pans immediately. Cool on wire racks.

Dilly-Onion Bread

Ingredients

- 1 **(¹/₄ oz.) pkg. dry yeast**
- ¹/₄ **cup warm water**
- 1 **cup small curd cottage cheese, room temperature**
- 1 **beaten egg**
- 2 **tablespoons sugar**
- 2 **tablespoons dill seed**
- 1 **teaspoon celery seed**
- 1 **tablespoon dried onions**
- 2¹/₄ **cups all-purpose flour**
- 1 **teaspoon salt**
- ¹/₄ **teaspoon baking soda**
- 2 **tablespoons melted butter**

Preparation

- In large mixing bowl, sprinkle yeast over warm water. Stir to dissolve. Mix in cottage cheese, egg, sugar, dill seed, celery seed and dried onions.
- Sift together flour, salt and baking soda. Add to cottage cheese mixture. Stir well. Cover. Let rise, in warm place, 1 hour or until double in size.
- Stir dough down and pour into well-buttered 8-inch round cake pan. Cover. Let rise about 45 minutes or until nearly double in size.
- Preheat oven in Convection Bake to 350°F (*325°F).
- Convection Bake for 35 to 40 minutes or until browned.
- Brush with melted butter and cool on wire rack.

*Note: Enter this temperature if your oven does not reduce the oven convection temperature automatically by 25°F in the display.

Cinnamon Bread

Ingredients

- 1/3 cup sugar
- 1 tablespoon salt
- 1/2 cup shortening
- 1 cup scalded milk
- 1/2 cup cold water
- 1 (1/4 oz.) pkg. dry yeast
- 1/4 cup warm water
- 1 beaten egg
- 5 1/2 to 6 cups all-purpose flour
- 2 tablespoons softened butter
- 1/2 cup sugar
- 4 teaspoons cinnamon

Preparation

- In large mixing bowl, combine 1/3 cup sugar, salt, shortening and hot milk. Stir until shortening melts. Add cold water.
- Dissolve yeast in warm water. Add to milk mixture. Add egg. Stir well.
- Add enough flour to form soft dough. Knead on floured surface 3 minutes until smooth. Place in large well-greased mixing bowl. Turn once to grease surface. Let rise 1 hour or until double in size.
- Punch dough down. Divide dough in half.
- On lightly floured surface, roll half of dough to 12" x 8" rectangle. Spread half of butter over dough.
- Combine 1/2 cup sugar and cinnamon. Sprinkle half of sugar mixture over buttered surface.
- Starting from long side, roll in jelly roll fashion. Repeat with remaining dough, butter and sugar mixture. Place on greased baking sheet and let rise until double in size.
- Preheat oven in Convection Bake to 375°F (*350°F).
- Convection Bake for 30 to 40 minutes or until golden brown.

Shortcake Biscuits

Ingredients

- 2 cups all-purpose flour
- 1/3 cup sugar
- 2 teaspoons baking powder
- 1/2 teaspoon baking soda
- 1/4 teaspoon salt
- 1/4 cup butter
- 1 cup whipping cream

Preparation

- Preheat oven in Convection Bake to 425°F (*400°F).
- In large mixing bowl, combine flour, sugar, baking powder, baking soda and salt. Using a pastry blender, cut in butter until mixture resembles coarse crumbs. Add cream. Stir until mixture forms stiff dough.
- Turn dough onto lightly floured surface. Knead to mix thoroughly. Roll out dough to 1/2-inch thickness.
- Using a floured 2-inch biscuit cutter, cut out biscuits. Place on ungreased cookie sheet, 1-inch apart.
- Convection Bake for 6 to 9 minutes or until biscuits are golden brown.

*Note: Enter this temperature if your oven does not reduce the oven convection temperature automatically by 25°F in the display.

Ingredients

- 2 cups Pillsbury BEST® All Purpose or Unbleached Flour
- 1/4 cup sugar
- 2 teaspoons baking powder
- 1/4 teaspoon salt
- 6 tablespoons butter
- 1/3 cup almond paste, cut into small pieces
- 1/2 cup milk
- 1/4 teaspoon almond extract
- 1 beaten egg

Preparation

- Preheat oven in Convection Bake to 400°F (*375°F).
- Lightly spray cookie sheet with nonstick cooking spray. Lightly spoon flour into measuring cup; level off. In large bowl, combine flour, sugar, baking powder and salt; mix well. With pastry blender or fork, cut in butter until mixture resembles coarse crumbs. Stir in almond paste, separating pieces to coat each with flour mixture.
- In small bowl, combine milk, almond extract and egg. Blend well. Add to flour mixture. Stir just until dry ingredients are moistened.
- On floured surface, gently knead dough about 6 times. Divide dough in half. Shape each into ball. Pat each ball into 5-inch round with center higher than edges. Cut each round into 6 wedges. Place wedges 1 inch apart on sprayed cookie sheet.
- Convection Bake for 10 to 15 minutes or until light golden brown. Cool 10 minutes before serving.

Variations

- **Basic Sweet**: Omit almond paste and almond extract.
- **Basic Non-Sweet**: Omit almond paste, almond extract and sugar.
- **Possible additions to basic sweet scones:** Chocolate chips, cinnamon chips, dried fruit.
- **Possible additions to basic non-sweet scones:** Nut, seeds, herbs, cheese, vegetables.

Reprinted with permission of Pillsbury Company. Adapted by General Electric for convection ovens.

BUTTERY BATTER BREAD   MAKES 1 LOAF

Ingredients

- 1 cup warm milk (110°F)
- 3/4 cup melted butter
- 1/4 cup sugar
- 1 1/2 teaspoons salt
- 1 (1/4 oz.) pkg. dry yeast
- 4 cups all-purpose flour, divided
- 4 slightly beaten eggs

Preparation

- In large mixing bowl, combine milk, butter, sugar and salt. Add yeast. Stir to dissolve. Add 2 cups flour and eggs. Beat with an electric mixer at medium speed 2 minutes until smooth. Stir in remaining 2 cups flour. Let rise 1 hour. Stir down and pour into well-greased, 10-inch tube pan. Cover. Let rise about 45 minutes or until double in size.
- Preheat oven in Convection Bake to 375°F (*350°F).
- Convection Bake for 25 to 30 minutes.

Note: Enter this temperature if your oven does not reduce the oven convection temperature automatically by 25°F in the display.

Cranberry-Glazed
Apple Dumpling—page 91

PEACH TORTE

Ingredients

- 3 tablespoons butter
- 1/2 cup firmly packed brown sugar
- 1 egg
- 1 teaspoon vanilla
- 3/4 cup all-purpose flour
- 1/4 teaspoon baking soda
- 1/4 teaspoon salt
- 1/2 cup milk
- 1/2 cup graham cracker crumbs
- 1/3 cup chopped pecans
- 1 cup peeled and sliced fresh peaches
- Pineapple juice
- 1 cup whipping cream

Preparation

- Preheat oven in Convection Bake to 325°F (*300°F).
- Grease bottom of 8-inch round cake pan and line with wax paper.
- In medium mixing bowl, cream butter and brown sugar with an electric mixer until light and fluffy. Add egg and vanilla. Stir well to blend. Gradually blend in flour, baking soda, salt and milk. Fold in cracker crumbs and pecans. Spread batter into pan.
- Convection Bake for 25 to 30 minutes.
- Cool on wire rack for 5 minutes. Invert onto wire rack and remove wax paper. Cool 10 minutes. Split cake into 2 layers.
- Brush fresh peaches with pineapple juice. Set aside.
- In small mixing bowl, beat whipping cream with an electric mixer until soft peaks form.
- Spread one-half of whipped cream on bottom layer and top with peach slices, reserving enough peach slices to garnish the top. Add remaining cake layer. Spread remaining whipped cream over top of cake and garnish with reserved peaches.
- Chill 2 hours before serving.

INCREDIBLE PEACH COBBLER

Ingredients

- 1/2 cup butter
- 1 (15.6 oz.) pkg. Pillsbury® Cranberry Quick Bread & Muffin Mix
- 2 tablespoons grated orange peel
- 2 (29 oz.) cans peach slices in light syrup, drained, reserving 1 cup liquid
- 1 egg
- 1/3 cup sweetened dried cranberries
- 1/3 cup sugar

Preparation

- Preheat oven in Convection Bake to 375°F (*350°F).
- Place butter in ungreased 13" x 9" pan. Place in oven until butter is melted. Remove from oven.
- Meanwhile, combine quick bread mix, 1 tablespoon of the orange peel, 1 cup reserved peach liquid and egg. Stir 50 to 75 strokes with spoon until mix is moistened. Drop mixture by spoonfuls over butter in pan. Spread slightly without stirring. Arrange peaches over mixture. Sprinkle with cranberries.
- In small bowl, combine sugar and remaining tablespoon orange peel. Mix well. Sprinkle over fruit.
- Convection Bake for 50 to 55 minutes or until edges are deep golden brown. Cool 20 minutes.
- Serve warm. Serve with vanilla ice cream, if desired.

Reprinted with permission of Pillsbury Company. Adapted by General Electric for convection ovens.

Note: Enter this temperature if your oven does not reduce the oven convection temperature automatically by 25°F in the display.

Ingredients

2 cups flour

$\frac{1}{2}$ cup sugar

$\frac{1}{2}$ teaspoon baking powder

6 tablespoons butter or shortening

4 eggs

1 teaspoon almond extract

$\frac{1}{2}$ cup chopped slivered almonds

Preparation

- Preheat oven in Convection Bake to 350°F (*325°F).

- Combine flour, sugar and baking powder. Cut in butter until mixture resembles coarse crumbs.

- Beat eggs until thick and light-colored. Add almond extract. Gradually beat egg mixture into flour mixture. Fold in almonds.

- Using #70 scoop or a teaspoon, drop cookies onto lightly greased baking sheets. Using a flat bottom glass dipped in flour or sugar, flatten cookies to $\frac{1}{4}$" thickness.

- Convection Bake for 12 to 14 minutes or until lightly browned. Remove cookies from oven, turn cookies over on cookie sheet and cool. After cookies are cool, place in oven and Convection Bake for 15 minutes.

Note: Cookies may be dipped in milk, wine or hot drinks (coffee, tea, etc.).

Variations

Brownie cookies: Increase sugar to $\frac{3}{4}$ cup, substitute vanilla for almond flavoring, add $\frac{1}{3}$ cup cocoa, $\frac{1}{2}$ cup mini chocolate chips and $\frac{1}{4}$ cup chopped walnuts.

Fruitcake cookies: Add $\frac{1}{4}$ teaspoon salt, $\frac{1}{3}$ cup white chocolate chips, $\frac{1}{2}$ cup dried chopped cherries and increase slivered almonds to $1\frac{1}{4}$ cups.

Reprinted with permission of Pillsbury Company. Adapted by General Electric for convection ovens.

***Note:** Enter this temperature if your oven does not reduce the oven convection temperature automatically by 25°F in the display.*

CHOCOLATE CHEESECAKE

Ingredients

CHEESECAKE

1¼ cups chocolate wafer crumbs

¼ cup melted butter

6 (1 oz.) squares semisweet chocolate

2 (8 oz.) pkgs. softened cream cheese

⅔ cup sugar

2 eggs

4 teaspoons Kahlúa

¾ teaspoon vanilla

1 cup sour cream

Brush chocolate on leaves. Chill until set.

CHOCOLATE LEAVES

½ cup semisweet chocolate chips

Non-poisonous, well-shaped leaves with no holes

Carefully peel leaf away from chocolate.

Preparation

CHEESECAKE

- Preheat oven in Convection Bake to 350°F (*325°F).
- In small mixing bowl, combine chocolate wafer crumbs and melted butter. Stir well. Press crumb mixture into bottom and sides of two 9-inch pie plates. Chill.
- Microwave chocolate squares on HIGH for 2 to 3 minutes until melted.
- Beat together cream cheese and sugar in mixing bowl with an electric mixer until light and fluffy. Beat in eggs, melted chocolate, Kahlúa and vanilla until smooth. Fold in sour cream. Pour mixture into crumb crust.
- Convection Bake for 30 to 40 minutes or until center is nearly set.
- Turn oven off and let cheesecake stand in oven 30 minutes with oven door ajar. Remove and cool on wire rack.
- Cover and chill at least 8 hours.
- Garnish with chocolate leaves.

CHOCOLATE LEAVES

- Microwave semisweet chocolate chips on HIGH for ½ to 1 minute until melted.
- Brush chocolate on leaves. Chill until set.
- Carefully peel leaf away from chocolate.

APPLE PIE

Ingredients

2 lbs. peeled and sliced baking apples

1 tablespoon lemon juice

¾ cup sugar

2 tablespoons all-purpose flour

1¼ teaspoons cinnamon

⅛ teaspoon nutmeg

⅛ teaspoon salt

Butter

Pastry for 2-crust (9-inch) pie

Preparation

- Preheat oven in Convection Bake to 425°F (*400°F).
- Toss sliced apples with lemon juice.
- Combine sugar, flour, cinnamon, nutmeg and salt. Add to apples and toss until well coated.
- Pour apple mixture into pastry-lined pie plate. Dot with butter. Top with remaining pastry and flute the edges. Slit top of pastry to vent.
- Convection Bake for 40 to 45 minutes or until golden brown.

***Note:** Enter this temperature if your oven does not reduce the oven convection temperature automatically by 25°F in the display.*

PEANUT BUTTER CARRUMBA BARS

Ingredients

CRUST

- 1 Pkg. Pillsbury Plus® Yellow Cake Mix
- ½ cup melted butter or margarine
- 1 egg
- 1 (6 oz.) pkg. (ten .6 oz. cups) chocolate-covered peanut butter cups, chopped

FILLING

- 1 (12.5 oz.) jar (1 cup) caramel ice cream topping
- ¼ cup peanut butter
- 2 tablespoons cornstarch
- ½ cup salted cocktail peanuts

TOPPING

- 1 can Pillsbury Milk Chocolate Frosting Supreme®
- 2 tablespoons mocha-flavored instant coffee beverage powder
- ½ cup chopped salted cocktail peanuts

Preparation

CRUST

- Preheat oven in Convection Bake to 350°F (*325°F).
- Combine all crust ingredients in mixing bowl. Beat at low speed until well blended. Lightly press in greased pan. Bake for 18 to 22 minutes or until light golden brown.

FILLING

- Combine all filling ingredients except peanuts in mixing bowl. Cook and stir over low heat until peanut butter is melted. Remove from heat. Stir in ½ cup peanuts. Spread evenly over crust. Return to oven and bake an additional 5 to 7 minutes or until almost set. Cool completely.

TOPPING

- In small bowl, combine frosting and beverage powder. Mix well. Spread over filling. Sprinkle with peanuts.

Reprinted with permission of Pillsbury Company. Adapted by General Electric for convection ovens.

FAVORITE CHERRY PIE

MAKES 8 SERVINGS

Ingredients

- 2 (16 oz.) cans pitted tart red cherries (water packed)
- 1 cup sugar
- ¼ cup cornstarch
- ½ teaspoon almond extract
- ⅛ teaspoon allspice
- ⅛ teaspoon nutmeg
- 1 tablespoon butter
- 6 drops red food coloring
  Pastry for 2-crust (9-inch) pie

Preparation

- Preheat oven in Convection Bake to 400°F (*375°F).
- Drain cherries, reserving 1 cup liquid.
- Combine reserved cherry liquid, sugar and cornstarch in a saucepan. Cook over medium heat until thickened and bubbly, stirring constantly. Cook and stir 2 minutes longer.
- Stir in drained cherries, almond extract, allspice, nutmeg, butter and food coloring. Cool. Pour cherry mixture into pastry-lined pie plate.
- Top with lattice crust. Seal and flute edges.
- Convection Bake for 35 to 45 minutes or until golden brown.

***Note:** Enter this temperature if your oven does not reduce the oven convection temperature automatically by 25°F in the display.*

CARAMEL BUNDT CAKE

Ingredients

CAKE

 1 (18 oz.) box yellow cake mix

 1/3 cup creamy peanut butter

 4 eggs

 3/4 cup water

 1/3 cup vegetable oil

 1/4 teaspoon vanilla

 1 cup chopped unsalted peanuts

 1 cup (6 oz.) semisweet chocolate chips

CARAMEL GLAZE

 2 tablespoons melted butter

 3/4 cup firmly packed brown sugar

 1 teaspoon cornstarch

 1/2 teaspoon butter flavoring

 1/4 cup whipping cream

 1/4 teaspoon vanilla

Preparation

• Preheat oven in Convection Bake to 375°F (*350°F).

• Combine cake mix, peanut butter, eggs, water, oil and vanilla in mixing bowl. Beat on medium speed for 3 minutes with an electric mixer.

• Pour 1/3 of the cake batter into greased and floured 12-cup Bundt pan. Sprinkle 1/3 cup peanuts and 1/3 cup chocolate chips over batter. Repeat with remaining batter, peanuts and chocolate chips, creating 3 layers

• Convection Bake for 40 to 45 minutes.

• Cool on wire rack for 10 minutes before removing from pan.

• Top with Caramel Glaze.

CARAMEL GLAZE

• Combine butter, brown sugar, cornstarch and butter flavoring in 4-cup glass measure. Mix until smooth. Gradually add whipping cream, stirring to blend.

• Microwave at HIGH 2 to 3 minutes until thickened. Stir in vanilla. Cool to room temperature.

• Makes 1 1/4 cups.

HOLIDAY PUMPKIN PIE

Ingredients

 1/2 cup firmly packed brown sugar

 1/2 cup all-purpose flour

 1/4 cup butter

 1/4 cup finely chopped pecans

 1 (16 oz.) can pumpkin

 1 cup firmly packed brown sugar

 1 tablespoon pumpkin pie spice

 1 tablespoon all-purpose flour

 1/2 teaspoon salt

 1 cup half and half

 2 beaten eggs

 Pastry for 1-crust (9-inch) pie

Preparation

• Preheat oven in Convection Bake to 375°F (*350°F).

• Combine 1/2 cup brown sugar and flour. Cut in butter until crumbly. Stir in nuts. Set aside.

• In large mixing bowl. Blend together pumpkin, 1 cup brown sugar, pumpkin pie spice, flour, salt, half and half and eggs. Pour filling into pastry-lined pie plate.

• Convection Bake for 45 to 50 minutes. Sprinkle with brown sugar-nut mixture and continue baking 10 to 15 minutes or until knife inserted near center comes out clean.

*Note: Enter this temperature if your oven does not reduce the oven convection temperature automatically by 25°F in the display.

LEMON COOLER COOKIES

Ingredients

1 cup softened butter
¹/₂ cup granulated sugar
1 tablespoon grated fresh lemon peel
1 egg
¹/₂ teaspoon lemon extract
¹/₂ teaspoon vanilla
2¹/₄ cups all-purpose flour
Granulated sugar
Powdered sugar

Preparation

- Preheat oven in Convection Bake to 375°F (*350°F).
- Cream butter and granulated sugar in medium mixing bowl with an electric mixer until light and fluffy. Beat in lemon peel, egg, lemon extract and vanilla. Gradually add flour and beat until blended.
- Using a #70 scoop or teaspoon, drop cookies onto shiny ungreased baking sheets.
- Dip bottom of 2¹/₂-inch round glass into sugar. Using bottom of glass, flatten to ¹/₄-inch thickness. Evenly space cookie sheets in oven cavity.
- Convection Bake for 9 to 12 minutes or until edges begin to brown.
- Remove cookies from pan and cool on wire racks.
- Sift powdered sugar over top.

Variations

Chocolate: Use ¹/₂ cup butter and ¹/₂ cup oil, increase sugar to ³/₄ cup, increase vanilla to 1 teaspoon, omit lemon peel and lemon extract, reduce flour to 2 cups, and add ¹/₄ cup cocoa.

Basic Sugar Cookie: Omit lemon peel and lemon extract, increase vanilla to 1 teaspoon, and increase sugar to 1 cup.

Pecan Sandies: Increase sugar to 1 cup, add 1¹/₂ teaspoons baking powder, ¹/₂ teaspoon salt and 1 cup chopped pecans.

Note: Enter this temperature if your oven does not reduce the oven convection temperature automatically by 25°F in the display.

PEANUTTY CHOCOLATE CHIP COOKIES

Ingredients

- 1 cup softened butter
- 1 cup firmly packed brown sugar
- 1/2 cup granulated sugar
- 1 1/3 cups (12 oz. jar) chunky peanut butter
- 1 egg
- 1 1/2 teaspoons vanilla
- 1 1/2 teaspoons butter flavoring
  Dash salt
- 1 1/2 cups all-purpose flour
- 2 cups (12 oz.) semisweet chocolate chips
- 1 cup chopped dry roasted peanuts

Preparation

- Preheat oven in Convection Bake to 350°F (*325°F).
- Cream butter, brown sugar and granulated sugar in medium mixing bowl with an electric mixer until fluffy.
- Add peanut butter, egg, vanilla, butter flavoring and salt. Continue to mix with an electric mixer until well blended.
- Stir in flour, chocolate chips and peanuts.
- For each cookie, place 1 tablespoon of dough onto lightly greased baking sheet; flatten to 1/4-inch thickness.
- Space cookies about 1/2-inch apart.
- Convection Bake for 12 to 14 minutes or until golden brown. Let stand 3 minutes. Remove to wire rack to cool.

PECAN CREAM ROLL

After baking, place cake on towel and roll together.

When cooled, unroll cake and spread with filling.

Ingredients

PECAN ROLL
- 4 eggs, separated
- 1 1/2 teaspoons vanilla
  Dash salt
- 1/2 cup granulated sugar
- 1/4 cup sifted all-purpose flour
- 3/4 cup finely chopped pecans
- Powdered sugar

FILLING
- 2 cups whipping cream
- 1/2 cup granulated sugar

Preparation

PECAN ROLL
- Preheat oven in Convection Bake to 375°F (*350°F).
- Beat egg whites, vanilla and salt in medium mixing bowl with an electric mixer until soft peaks form. Gradually add granulated sugar, beating until stiff peaks form.
- Beat egg yolks until thick and lemon colored. Fold beaten egg yolks into whites. Carefully fold in flour and pecans.
- Spread batter evenly into greased and floured 15" x 10" x 1" jelly roll pan.
- Convection Bake for 9 to 11 minutes. Immediately loosen sides and turn out onto towel sprinkled with powdered sugar. Starting at narrow end, roll cake and towel together. Cool on wire rack.
- Unroll cake and spread with 3/4 of filling. Roll cake and use remaining filling to decorate top. Chill.

FILLING
- Beat whipping cream in medium mixing bowl, until soft peaks form.
- Add granulated sugar and continue beating until firm.

Note: Enter this temperature if your oven does not reduce the oven convection temperature automatically by 25°F in the display.

PECAN CRISPS

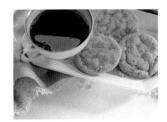

Ingredients

- 2¹/₂ cups firmly packed brown sugar
- 1 cup softened butter
- 1 teaspoon vanilla
- 2 eggs
- 3 cups all-purpose flour
- ¹/₂ teaspoon baking soda
- 1 cup toasted chopped pecans
- 3 tablespoons sugar

Preparation

- Preheat oven in Convection Bake to 375°F (*350°F).
- Combine brown sugar and butter. Beat until well blended. Add vanilla and eggs. Blend well. Add flour, baking soda and pecans. Mix well.
- Shape dough into 1-inch balls. Place 2-inches apart on ungreased cookie sheets.
- Flatten to ¹/₈-inch thickness with bottom of glass dipped in 3 tablespoons sugar.
- Convection Bake for 6 to 10 minutes or until edges are light golden brown. Cool 1 minute. Remove from cookie sheets. Cool 2 minutes or until completely cooled.

Reprinted with permission of Pillsbury Company. Adapted by General Electric for convection ovens.

MOONBEAM COOKIES

Ingredients

- 1 (18 oz.) pkg. Pillsbury® Refrigerated Sugar Cookies
- 1 cup coconut
- ¹/₂ cup lemon curd (from 10 oz. jar)**
- 2 oz. vanilla-flavored candy coating or ¹/₃ cup white vanilla chips

Preparation

- Preheat oven in Convection Bake to 350°F (*325°F).
- Break up cookie dough. Stir in coconut. Shape dough into 1-inch balls. Place 2-inches apart on ungreased cookie sheets.
- With thumb or handle of wooden spoon, make indentation in center of each cookie. Spoon about ¹/₂ teaspoon lemon curd into each indentation.
- Convection Bake for 10 to 13 minutes or until edges are light golden brown. Remove from cookie sheets. Cool 5 minutes.
- Microwave candy coating in small microwave-safe bowl on MEDIUM for 2 minutes. Stir well.
- Drizzle over cookies.

**Note: Lemon pie filling can be substituted for lemon curd.

Reprinted with permission of Pillsbury Company. Adapted by General Electric for convection ovens.

*Note: Enter this temperature if your oven does not reduce the oven convection temperature automatically by 25°F in the display.

Ingredients

- ¾ **cup sugar**
- ½ **cup softened margarine or butter**
- 2 **teaspoons almond extract**
- 3 **eggs**
- 3 **cups all-purpose flour**
- 2 **teaspoons baking powder**
- ½ **cup chopped candied cherries**
- ½ **cup miniature chocolate chips**
- 3 **tablespoons melted chocolate chips, optional**
- 3 **tablespoons melted white vanilla chips, optional**

Preparation

- Preheat oven in Convection Bake to 375°F (*350°F).
- Lightly grease cookie sheet.
- Combine sugar and margarine. Beat until well blended. Add almond extract and eggs. Blend well. Add flour and baking powder. Mix well. Stir in cherries and miniature chocolate chips.
- Shape dough into two 10-inch rolls. Place rolls 5 inches apart on greased cookie sheet. Flatten each to 3 inches wide.
- Convection Bake for 20 to 25 minutes or until set and light golden brown. Remove from cookie sheet and place on wire racks. Cool 10 minutes.
- With serrated knife, cut rolls diagonally into ½-inch thick slices. Arrange slices, cut side down, on ungreased cookie sheets.
- Convection Bake for 8 to 10 minutes or until bottoms begin to brown. Turn cookies over and bake an additional 5 minutes or until browned and crisp. Remove from cookie sheets. Cool 15 minutes or until completely cooled.
- Drizzle cookies with melted chocolate and vanilla chips.
- Store in tightly covered container.

Reprinted with permission of Pillsbury Company. Adapted by General Electric for convection ovens.

Note: *Enter this temperature if your oven does not reduce the oven convection temperature automatically by 25°F in the display.*

MISSISSIPPI MUD CAKE

Ingredients

CAKE

- 1 (1 lb. 2.25 oz.) pkg. Pillsbury® Moist Supreme® Devil's Food Cake Mix
- 1¼ cups water
- ½ cup oil
- 3 eggs
- 1 cup chopped pecans
- 1 (7 oz.) jar marshmallow creme

FROSTING

- 1 (16 oz.) can chocolate fudge frosting
- 1 to 2 tablespoons milk

Preparation

CAKE

- Preheat oven in Convection Bake to 350°F (*325°F).
- Grease and flour bottom only of 13" x 9" pan.
- Combine cake mix, water, oil and eggs in large mixing bowl. Beat at low speed until moistened. Beat 2 minutes at medium speed. Pour batter into greased and floured pan. Sprinkle pecans evenly over batter.
- Convection Bake for 30 to 40 minutes or until toothpick inserted in center comes out clean. Remove cake from oven.
- Spoon marshmallow creme evenly over top of hot cake.
- Carefully spread to cover cake. Cool cake 15 minutes.

FROSTING

- Combine frosting and enough milk for desired spreading consistency. Blend well.
- Drop frosting by spoonfuls onto cake. Spread gently to cover. Lightly swirl to marble. Cool 1 hour or until completely cooled.

Reprinted with permission of Pillsbury Company. Adapted by General Electric for convection ovens.

Note: Enter this temperature if your oven does not reduce the oven convection temperature automatically by 25°F in the display.

PINEAPPLE UPSIDE-DOWN CAKE

Ingredients

- ½ cup firmly packed brown sugar
- ¼ cup melted margarine or butter
- 6 canned pineapple slices, drained
- 6 maraschino cherries
- 2 eggs, separated
- ½ cup sugar
- ¾ cup Pillsbury BEST® All Purpose or Unbleached Flour
- ½ teaspoon baking powder
- ¼ teaspoon salt
- ¼ cup pineapple juice
  Whipped cream

Preparation

- Preheat oven in Convection Bake to 350°F (*325°F).
- Combine brown sugar and melted margarine or butter in small bowl. Blend well. Spread in bottom of ungreased 9-inch round cake pan. Arrange pineapple slices and maraschino cherries over brown sugar mixture. Set aside.
- Beat egg yolks until thick and lemon colored. Gradually add sugar. Beat well.
- Add flour, baking powder, salt and pineapple juice. Mix well.
- Beat egg whites until stiff peaks form. Fold into batter. Pour batter evenly over pineapple slices and cherries.
- Convection Bake for 25 to 30 minutes or until toothpick inserted in center comes out clean. Cool upright in pan 2 minutes.
- Invert cake onto serving plate. Serve warm with whipped cream.

Reprinted with permission of Pillsbury Company. Adapted by General Electric for convection ovens.

GINGER-APPLE CRISP

Ingredients

- ⅓ cup corn flake crumbs
- ¼ cup firmly packed brown sugar
- 3 tablespoons Pillsbury BEST® All Purpose or Unbleached Flour
- 2 tablespoons chopped crystallized ginger or 1 teaspoon ginger
- 2 tablespoons melted margarine or butter
- 6 cups (approx. 6 medium) thinly sliced peeled apples
- 2 tablespoons sugar
- 2 teaspoons lemon juice

Preparation

- Preheat oven in Convection Bake to 400°F (*375°F).
- Spray 2-quart casserole with nonstick cooking spray.
- In small bowl, combine corn flake crumbs, brown sugar, flour and ginger. Mix well. Add margarine. Stir until well mixed.
- Place apples in sprayed casserole. Add sugar and lemon juice. Toss to coat.
- Sprinkle apples with crumb mixture. Press gently.
- Convection Bake for 25 to 30 minutes or until apples are tender and mixture is bubbly.
- Cool slightly. If desired, serve warm with ice cream.

Reprinted with permission of Pillsbury Company. Adapted by General Electric for convection ovens.

***Note:** Enter this temperature if your oven does not reduce the oven convection temperature automatically by 25°F in the display.*

CRANBERRY-GLAZED APPLE DUMPLING

Ingredients

- **1** Pillsbury® Refrigerated Pie Crust (from 15-oz. pkg.), softened as directed on package
- **4** medium peeled and cored baking apples
- **2** tablespoons cream cheese
- **2** tablespoons sweetened dried cranberries
- **1** tablespoon sugar
- **1/4** teaspoon cinnamon
- **1 1/2** cups raspberry-cranberry juice drink
- **2/3** cup sugar

Preparation

- Preheat oven in Convection Bake to 400°F (*375°F).

- Unfold pie crust, peel off top plastic sheet. Press out fold lines. Cut crust into 8 wedges with kitchen scissors or knife.

- Place 2 crust wedges together at points, overlapping points about 1/2-inch. Press to seal. Center 1 apple on overlapped points. Spoon about 1/2 tablespoon each of the cream cheese and cranberries into apple. Repeat with remaining wedges and apples.

- Combine 1 tablespoon sugar and 1/4 teaspoon cinnamon in small bowl. Sprinkle each apple with 1/4 teaspoon sugar-cinnamon mixture. (Reserve remaining mixture.)

- Make 1 cut in each crust wedge from apple to edge to make 4 strips per apple. Separate strips enough to space evenly around apple. Bring strips up around apple, overlapping and sealing at top.

- Place wrapped apples in ungreased 8-inch square (2-quart) glass baking dish.

- Combine juice drink and 2/3 cup sugar in small saucepan. Bring to a boil, stirring well to dissolve sugar. Pour over wrapped apples in baking dish. Sprinkle apples with remaining sugar-cinnamon mixture.

- Convection Bake for 20 to 30 minutes or until apples are almost tender and crust is deep golden brown. Spoon sauce mixture from baking dish over each apple. Bake an additional 5 to 10 minutes or until apples are fork-tender. Cool at least 1 hour before serving.

- Serve dumplings in shallow dessert dishes. Spoon sauce over dumplings.

Reprinted with permission of Pillsbury Company. Adapted by General Electric for convection ovens.

__Note:__ Enter this temperature if your oven does not reduce the oven convection temperature automatically by 25°F in the display.

Ingredients

- **1 (19.5 oz.) pkg. Pillsbury® Rich & Moist Fudge Brownie Mix**
- **¹/₂ cup melted butter or margarine**
- **¹/₄ cup water**
- **2 eggs**
- **2 cups quick-cooking rolled oats**
- **2 cups chopped walnuts**
- **1 (12 oz.) pkg. (2 cups) semisweet chocolate chips**
- **1 (14 oz.) can sweetened condensed milk**

Preparation

- Preheat oven in Convection Bake to 350°F (*325°F).
- Grease 13" x 9" pan.
- Combine brownie mix, butter, water and eggs. Beat 50 strokes with spoon. Add oats and walnuts. Mix well.
- In medium bowl, combine chocolate chips and condensed milk. Microwave on HIGH for 1¹/₂ minutes or until chips are melted and mixture is smooth, stirring twice.
- Spread half of brownie batter in greased pan. Spread chocolate mixture over batter. Drop remaining brownie mixture by teaspoonfuls over chocolate layer. Brownie mixture will not completely cover chocolate layer.
- Convection Bake for 20 to 25 minutes or until brownie topping feels dry and edges begin to pull away from sides of pan. DO NOT OVERBAKE.
- Cool 2 hours. Refrigerate 1¹/₂ hours.
- Cut into bars. Serve cold or at room temperature. Store in refrigerator.

Reprinted with permission of Pillsbury Company. Adapted by General Electric for convection ovens.

Note: Enter this temperature if your oven does not reduce the oven convection temperature automatically by 25°F in the display.

BASIC PASTRY SHELL

Ingredients

- **1 cup unsifted all-purpose flour**
- **½ teaspoon salt**
- **6 tablespoon shortening**
- **2 tablespoons ice water**

Preparation

- Preheat oven in Convection Bake to 450°F (*425°F).
- Combine flour and salt. Cut in shortening with a pastry blender until mixture resembles the size of small peas. Sprinkle water over flour-shortening mixture. Stir with fork to form ball.
- Roll out on floured pastry cloth with rolling pin to ⅛" thickness. Let stand a few minutes before shaping.
- Line a 9-inch pie plate with pastry dough shaping to the edge of pie plate. Prick pastry with fork.
- Convection Bake for 9 to 12 minutes. Pastry is done when it looks dry and blistered and is not doughy.

Variation

If desired, 3 tablespoons cold butter and 3 tablespoons shortening may be used for more flavor and color.

CRUMB PIE SHELL

Ingredients

- **¼ cup butter**
- **1¼ cups fine cookie crumbs (vanilla wafer, graham cracker, chocolate wafer, gingersnaps, etc.)**
- **2 tablespoons sugar**

Preparation

- Preheat oven in Convection Bake to 375°F (*350°F).
- Place butter in a 9-inch pie plate. Microwave at HIGH (10) for 30 seconds or until melted.
- Blend in crumbs and sugar. Reserve 2 tablespoons of crumb mixture for garnish.
- Press crumb mixture firmly and evenly into 9-inch pie plate.
- Convection Bake at 350°F for 8 to 10 minutes.

*Note: Enter this temperature if your oven does not reduce the oven convection temperature automatically by 25°F in the display.

Ingredients

- ½ **cup water**
- ¼ **cup margarine or butter**
- ½ **cup all-purpose flour**
- ¼ **teaspoon salt**
- 2 **eggs**

Preparation

- Preheat oven in Convection Bake to 425°F (*400°F).

- Combine water and margarine. Bring to boil over medium heat. Stir in flour and salt. Cook, stirring vigorously until mixture leaves sides of pan in smooth ball. Remove from heat. Add eggs one at a time, beating vigorously after each addition until mixture is smooth and glossy.

- Spoon 6 mounds of dough (about ¼ cup each) 3 inches apart onto ungreased cookie sheet.

- Convection Bake for 15 to 20 minutes or until golden brown. Remove from oven.

- Prick puffs with sharp knife to allow steam to escape. Remove from cookie sheet. Cool 1 hour or until completely cooled.

- Split cream puffs, if desired, remove any filaments of soft dough. Fill with ice cream, whipped cream or pudding. If desired, top with chocolate sauce, other dessert toppings or nuts.

Cooking Tip

An electric mixer at medium speed can be used to beat in eggs. Beat for 1 minute after each addition until smooth and glossy. DO NOT OVERBEAT.

Variations

Eclairs: Drop cream puff dough into 12 long ovals about 1-inch wide. Convection Bake for 10 to 15 minutes. When cool, fill with prepared vanilla pudding and drizzle with a chocolate glaze. Makes 12 Eclairs.

Snack Cream Puffs: Drop dough by tablespoonfuls, making 20 small cream puffs. Convection Bake 10 to 15 minutes. Makes 20 Cream Puffs.

Praline Cream Puffs: Prepare and bake 6 cream puffs as directed above. When cool, fill with vanilla ice cream. Drizzle with warm caramel ice cream topping. Sprinkle with chopped pecans.

*****Note:** Enter this temperature if your oven does not reduce the oven convection temperature automatically by 25°F in the display.

INDEX